G000277625

RESEI

MY NEW FOREST HOME

Cover: The author with owl.

Overleaf: Len Witt with his cow Dolly.

JOHN SEARL.

My
New Forest
Home

Irene Soper

Illustrations by John Searl

EX LIBRIS PRESS

Published in 1996 by
EX LIBRIS PRESS
1 The Shambles
Bradford on Avon
Wiltshire

Cover printed by Shires Press, Trowbridge
Printed and bound by Cromwell Press,
Melksham, Wiltshire

Design and typesetting by
Ex Libris Press

Typeset in 10 point Palatino

ISBN 0 948578 81 5

CONTENTS

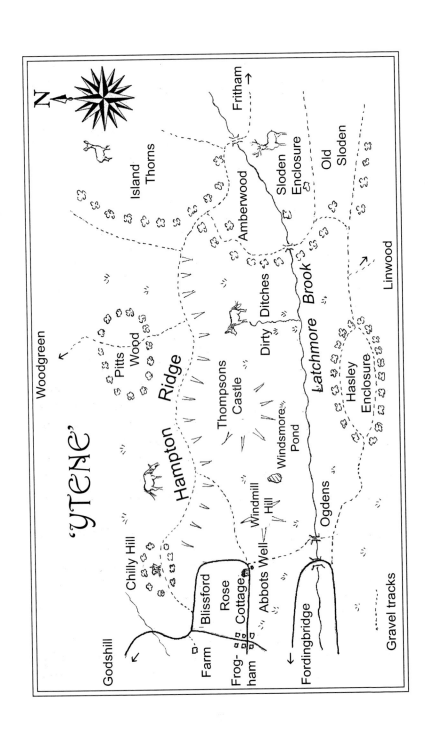

Introduction

THE NEW FOREST IS A unique tract of land situated in the county of Hampshire. Comprising some 38,000 hectares, or 1330 square miles, it reaches from the Wiltshire border southward to the coast. Despite the name 'New', it is one of our oldest forests.

The soil is very acid being derived from blue clay overlaid by sand and gravel and differs from the chalklands to the north. The vegetation therefore has adapted to the conditions; plants such as bracken, gorse, and heather are typical.

The management of the New Forest is divided, with the Forestry Commission responsible for the maintenance of the woodlands, open heath, and the preservation of the wildlife whilst the Verderers look after the welfare of the commoners and the grazing for their domestic animals. The title Verderer is derived from the Norman word vert meaning green and referring to the woodlands.

The verderers, of which there are ten, sit in open court at Lyndhurst every two months on a Monday. Any member of the public who has a grievance can exercise an ancient custom dating from the Court of Swainmote by making a 'presentment'. They are invited to do so by the senior Agister who, wearing his official livery, riding breeches and green jacket, and standing in the Court's old wooden dock raises his right hand and calls out:

"Oyez, oyez, oyez!
All manner of persons who have any presentment or matter or thing to do at this Court of Swainmote, let him come forward and he shall be heard! God Save The Queen!"

This ancient Court of Swainmote has been held for centuries in the Verderers' Hall at Lyndhurst, the Forest's capital. The Hall was built in 1388 either beside or within the manor house of the Royal Manor of Lyndhurst. The old entrance was at one time through the Tudor porch but was altered during changes to the Hall and Queens House in 1851.

Ytene, the Saxon word for a furzy waste, referred to the forest of pre-Norman times. The land was just acres of gorse and heather with a scattering of poor woodland, and it was inhabited by peasants or *churls* as they were then called. Their primitive dwellings were built of waffle and daub on a wood frame with a floor of mud. The only light came through the open door and a hole in the roof which let the smoke escape. Sticks were burnt on a hearthstone in the middle of the room to provide heat.

A few swine were owned by the *churl* which at certain times of the year he would turn into the woods to feed. Sometimes a small flock of sheep would be kept in pens built of hurdles and stones. These pens were essential as protection against the wolves that roamed freely over the countryside in those days. It was not an uncommon sight to see the peasants armed with spears, their faithful hounds at their sides, go crashing through the undergrowth chasing the hungry wolves away from their flocks.

A Saxon homestead was a little more elaborate. There would have been a large hall of timber construction, its overhead rafters blackened with soot from the fire below. A few brightly woven rugs might have decorated the walls with skins scattered on the floor. The furniture probably consisted of a trestle table and benches placed around the walls.

There is proof of an earlier habitation of *Ytene* by the relics left behind. The Bronze Age round burrows are numerous, and one or two small hilltop forts are believed to be from the Iron Age. Fragments of lovely Roman pottery can easily be found thrown up by moles, or dug out by badgers, remains from the pottery industry which flourished during the Roman occupation in the third and fourth centuries.

But it was William the Conqueror who declared in 1079 that all the land which lay between Southampton Water and the Avon Valley, the Solent and the Wiltshire Downs was in future to be his own exclusive hunting ground. So the New Forest was established. The peasants were forbidden to fence their land lest it should interfere with the movement of the deer and to compensate they were given common right to graze their domestic animals throughout the Forest. This right together with others has survived the years and is still practiced today.

Living in the New Forest is a singular experience as my husband Arthur and I were to discover when we moved to our cottage at Abbots Well. Where else will you meet ponies, cattle and pigs wandering freely along the roads, or encounter a group of ponies galloping across the heath and through the village pursued by shouting horsemen cracking whips during the annual round-ups.

Leaving our respective counties behind us, Arthur's Cornwall, and my Wiltshire, we made the New Forest our home which we have enjoyed for some thirty years.

The book which follows is an attempt to relate our experiences and happenings along the way, to tell of the people and a way of life in the Forest which differs from any other and to explain some of the traditions and customs still carried out.

CS

1 Abbots Well

THE SMALL THATCHED COTTAGE WITH its pink-washed walls nestles peacefully on the side of the hill in a quiet corner of the New Forest at Abbots Well near the village of Frogham. For over three hundred years it has provided a home for generations of foresters, and in recent times for artists, writers, and lastly herbalist and writer Juliette de Bairacli-Levy. When Juliette lived there the cottage was in a wild garden. Tall grasses hid the bee skeps and old twisted apple trees bent double under their loads. When she departed the cottage remained empty and our now modern house was built in part of the garden. The cottage has a wealth of history as I will relate later and was fortunately saved from demolition on conditions that it was used only as an outhouse.

We took possession of our house and cottage in springtime when the apple trees were in full blossom. It is a peaceful place as the nearest main road lies some two miles distant. The most likely noise to be heard from the lane is the sound of horses' hooves, the crisp clinking of the shod ponies with riders, and the more gentle, less hurried footsteps of the forest ponies as they amble to and fro. In the garden silver birches and willows surround the house but none too thick or tall to keep out the sun.

From the house the numerous large windows give us uninterrupted views across the open moorland of Hampton Ridge and a small ridge called Chilly Hill. In spring and summer these hills are in turn golden and purple with gorse and heather then bronze with the autumn bracken.

Outside in the lane, under a bank of fern and bracken and shaded by a single birch tree, are the ancient wells of Abbots Well – one an open tub from which the animals drink, the other is brick-lined with a wooden lid. It is only in recent times that the covered well was bricked; originally it was a wooden tub the same as the other. Within the last few years the Forestry Commission have erected an oak fence partly around the wells to protect them from vehicles which take the corner too wide.

Little is known of the origin of the wells but they are mentioned in New Forest chronicles as early as 1217. The belief is that as Frogham had Roman connections there is possibly some link between the Roman period and the wells. One thing certain is the coolness, freshness and health-giving qualities of the water. Many people stop at the wells to quench their thirst, or fill containers to take the water away. At one time an old forester from the village used to collect his water daily in pails suspended from an old fashioned yoke across his shoulders.

It has been my delight to watch from the window the ponies drinking usually early morning with the first rays of sun lighting up the rich colours of their shaggy coats. Only a short time after we came to Abbots Well, twenty-five donkeys arrived, all hustling and pushing for their turn to drink the cool clear water. Not only ponies and donkeys but a variety of animals come to the wells to quench their thirsts. One summer evening when a thick drizzle swept across the hills, keeping the Forest peaceful and quiet from human intrusion, a white buck carrying a very fine head slowly walked past the garden gate. He paused for a few seconds at the well to sip the cool water before climbing the bank and vanishing from sight in the long bracken. On another occasion, when a soft rain was falling a herd of fallow deer surrounded the well before they too disappeared into the undergrowth.

Beyond the wells on the open Forest is a small rise called Windmill Hill, on the other side of which lies Windsmore Pond. A charming little pond fringed here and there with reeds and completely surrounded by a soft springy turf; in fact the bottom of the whole pond is grass. There are no fish or other marine life for in hot weather the water disappears.

The Forest around the pond is wild and swept frequently by the winds that blow uninterrupted for miles across the undulating moorland of gorse and heather. This 'furzy waste' stretches to the distant horizon where it meets the ancient yews of Sloden.

When we first moved to Abbots Well there was a lush water meadow adjoining the garden on the north side. Owing to numerous springs the field was constantly damp, and in places boggy. This situation made the meadow a place little visited by people, it became one of nature's wild gardens. One person who did come to the field on occasions, well equipped with big boots to negotiate the mud and binder twine to secure the gate, was Len Witt. Len was a forester neighbour who kept one cow called Dolly of which he was very fond. He brought Dolly down the lane every day to graze in the meadow. As Len wore hobnailed boots he could always be heard well before he appeared over the hill. His brown cow Dolly following behind him on the end of a rope had a mournful look with one horn turned upwards and the other turned down. When we got to know them better they both proved to be great characters. Len always stopped and watered his cow at the well before putting her into the meadow. The five-bar gate which was completely suspended on twine usually took him twenty minutes to open by the time he had untied all the knots, and the same time to replace it; the field did not make a very good grazing place as the damp boggy ground bred the vicious stinging flies that torment the poor animals.

The meadow, which was divided into two by a hedge of willows had become overgrown and the reeds in the boggy parts grew tall. In spring the cotton fluff from the willows floated in the wind, carpeting the garden and surrounding countryside.

Wild daffodils grew in clumps under the hedges and, later, marsh marigolds appeared with wild flags amongst the rushes. A host of other wild flowers and herbs were to be found in the long grasses ragged robin, meadow-sweet, cuckoo flowers and, here and there, the marsh orchid. Later in the summer the whole meadow was covered with buttercups. Around the edges of the field in the watery ditches wild mint grew. Perhaps once long ago the peasant gathered it from here to make the ancient Forest drink called Hum Beer.

When the sun grew hot the dragonflies began their restless dance, hovering and darting from plant to plant, gathering energy from the heat that sent all other creatures into a midday lull. Then the butterflies rested with outstretched wings on some of the more pungent smelling flowers and plants, and the colourful little cinnebar moths took their siesta on their favourite ragwort flowers.

The road hedge was comprised mainly of stately oaks growing out of a tangled mass of blackthorn, brambles, wild rose bushes and holly, so thick and deep as to be impenetrable from either side. The path through the gate led into a small copse; there amongst the willows three old apple trees grew. Unpruned for years they had grown long and twisted, the branches in places touching the ground but still bearing a crop of delicious apples. Beneath the branches of the apple trees, half hidden by the long grass, were several bee hives, the bees from which had at their disposal the blossom from the trees, the flowers in the meadow and garden, as well as the heather in the forest beyond.

At the far end of the meadow there was a drier patch of ground and it was here that Len grew rhubarb and cabbages. The meadow was crisscrossed with various animal tracks. Badgers had well worn paths leading to and from the garden which they used on night visits. Foxes also did their hunting in the long grass stalking mice and baby rabbits and other small rodents, leaping and pouncing just like a cat teasing a mouse. Condemned as a villain for stealing chicken it is often overlooked that the fox helps the farmer in this way.

Rabbit burrows were to be found in the banks, especially under the garden. At dusk and early morning the young rabbits would come onto the lawn and eat the grass. One evening just before dark, when one very small rabbit was having his last nibble, a tawny owl swooped from the yew tree overhead but the rabbit was the quicker of the two and jumped to the safe cover of the tall plants in the flower border. They have not always been so lucky especially if a vixen has been hunting, for when cubs were around she would come from her earth in the neighbouring field just as the sun was setting and stalk stealthily along the bank to the beehives, invariably returning ten minutes later with a rabbit in her mouth.

Another enemy of the rabbit also lurking in the long grass being so quick and small and seldom seen is the weasel, similar in colour to the fox, and equal in guile. My husband tells the story of how one day when he was sitting quietly by a pond fishing a fox came along to the edge of the water and proceeded to lie on its back waving all four legs in the air trying to attract the ducks to come within striking range. I encountered a weasel in the meadow doing a similar thing. A fallen branch lay along the grass and the weasel was running to and fro standing up on two legs and pawing the air and doing all manner of antics. This performance it kept up for nearly a quarter of an hour, all for the benefit of a hedge sparrow that was feeding nearby, in an attempt to entice it closer.

Not long after this I saw a weasel take a rabbit in the meadow. My attention was drawn by the terrified screams of the rabbit as it was caught at the back of the neck and dragged by the weasel across the field. By the time that I left the house and reached the road beside the field the rabbit was already lying dead in the ditch, and the wicked little face of the weasel was watching me from the undergrowth in the hedge.

In high summer, when the heavily leafed branches of the willows touched the ground giving lots of cover, a roe deer would sometimes venture into the field, quietly and gently feeding. On hearing a noise it would freeze and stand motionless, sometimes for nearly an hour at a time, blending in with the background to become almost invisible.

The meadow, being marshy ground, was a favourite place also for adders. On a sunny day you might find one curled up asleep on the bank. Occasionally, when seeking new ground, they would pass through the garden. Their colours varied considerably, ranging from a light olive-green to a dark chocolate-brown bordering on black, to match the habitat in which they lived.

Keeping the meadow constantly live was a variety of bird life. Wood pigeons flapped from tree to tree and a pair of great green woodpeckers in a hole of an old bent tree trunk advertised their presence every time they came back to the nest by their strident note. Cuckoos would call and answer each other at intervals throughout the day until at dusk a hen-bird would come to roost in a holly tree outside the window, giving a completely different tune just as it entered the tree.

As summer mellowed into autumn and the leaves on the oaks turned yellow the squirrels busily collected acorns and hazel nuts to bury ready for winter.

Our first summer at Abbots Well passed very quickly and after such a short time we realized that all we had dreamed of was there. It was peaceful but at the same time alive with activity, with ponies and cattle coming and going in the lane, people visiting the wells for water, and particularly the twice daily trips of Len Witt with his cow Dolly for her drink at the well. Spread before us was the open Forest with nothing man-made as far as you could see. It presented ground to be explored, with pools, trickling streams and peat bogs, earths and setts, and an abundance of wild life to be discovered – a soil and vegetation so different from the chalkland we had left behind but equal in its beauty.

2 The Old Forest Cottage

ONE OF THE DELIGHTS OF our new Abbots Well home was the little thatched cottage standing in a corner of the garden, half hidden by overgrown laurels and a spreading yew tree. Built of cob, it is believed to be over three hundred years old. The walls outside were a faded pink, and the thatched roof had been pulled to pieces by the birds. The inside of the cottage consisted of one big room, with a small alcove kitchen. It was the remains of a typical old New Forest dwelling of former days.

In its original state the cottage had an upstairs room reached by a ladder-type stairway. The room beneath had a very low ceiling which must have made it dark in wintertime. In recent years the height of the downstairs ceiling had been raised, thereby disposing of the upper room. At some time the chimney stack had fallen in and been thatched over and the fireplace boarded up.

By talking to forester neighbours we discovered later that at one time the building had been longer. As well as the living quarters it had a place known as the 'shop' where the animal food was kept and a turf store all under one roof. Outside, attached to the end of the buildings, were the pigsties. The fact that there was a turf store for keeping the fuel for the big open fireplace indicates that the cottage had the rights of Turbary. This meant that the forester living in the cottage had the entitlement to go into the forest and cut the turf, which is a kind of peat, for his fire.

When the cottage came into our possession it had been used as a log store; it smelt damp and musty with cobwebs hanging in every corner. Our first task of tidying up the old cabin was to clear away the entangled undergrowth that entwined the outside of it. We cut the overhanging laurels to let the sun in and spent days hacking away the brambles, digging up roots and sawing up laurel branches. An old dead apple tree had to be cut down; this provided us with a pile of logs for burning. Each evening after a day's hard work it was pleasant to relax in front of a log fire with its fragrant applewood smoke. Whilst cutting away the laurel and brambles we found the remains of the old original garden gate that once opened onto a small path leading to the cottage door.

CB

Now that the outside was clear we started on the inside of the cottage. The cobwebs were thick upon the once white walls and hung about the windows like grey curtains. In every corner spiders were peering out of their webs waiting for any unsuspecting fly to be caught in their sticky traps. On the tiled floor black beetles scurried away seeking refuge in the many holes.

The air was heavy with the smell of rotting wood where for so long the room had been stacked with moss and lichen-covered logs. Being early autumn the weather was still warm so we opened the door and windows to let the warm air find its way in before setting about the task of cleaning up. After a day or so of hard work the inside of the cottage began to look a little more like a living room and less like a wood store. All that was needed then was a coat of whitewash, but not before the fireplace had been opened up, a long and dirty job.

The fireplace had held a great attraction to us since first looking inside the cottage. We longed to know what lay behind the piece of white board that blocked up the front of it and judging by the age of the building there must be a large chimney piece somewhere behind it all.

The board came down quite easily only to expose a big iron stove with a brick surround. It took Arthur several evenings of hard work with a sledge hammer to remove it only to find another pile of rubble and bricks where at some time the chimney had fallen inwards. It took many trips with the wheelbarrow to take it all away, but when it was eventually cleared it revealed an old inglenook fireplace with the remains of a baking oven in the wall. On the opposite side, the wall was curved where it had once been an alcove for a seat. The resting backs of many a forester had polished the bricks quite smooth.

Hanging from a beam halfway up the open chimney was an old rusty chain with a hook on the end for iron pots, just as it was in the days when they cooked over an open fire. It took Arthur weeks to restore the fireplace using some of the old bricks. When finished it was really worth all the work and patience put into it.

We gave the outside of the thick cob wall a pink wash, and asked the local thatcher if he would patch and wire the thatch. We were fortunate to have a master thatcher living in the village. Eventually the day was fixed for him to come. It was a beautiful morning, the sun rose dear and bright, and the thatcher and his mate arrived early. They said they would have preferred a wet day as the straw needed to be constantly damped down. It took them a week to remove the top layer of old wheaten straw, re-thatch, and wire.

During the evening of the day that the thatcher finished we noticed a sparrow with a beak full of food frantically trying to get under the wire into the thatch. It was then we realized there was a nest with young in it under a beam beneath the new thatch and wire. Something had to be done quickly as the young birds had already been without food for some hours. So without delay Arthur put up the ladder and lifted the wire sufficiently for the sparrow to go in and out with food.

We were delighted to discover not long after coming to live at Abbots Well that. In the 1950s, herbalist and writer Juliette de Bairacli Levy had lived in the cottage with her two children whilst working on her herbal remedies. Later she wrote a book about her stay in the forest cottage entitled *Wanderers in the New Forest*. A colourful character, Juliette had gypsies for friends as well as artists such as French painter George Brunon and Augustus John. The latter's lovely wife Dorelia came on occasions to visit the cottage from her nearby home 'Fryen Court'. Dorelia dressed in one of her long skirts and Juliette wearing perhaps her big apron with all its pockets, talking together in the wild garden by the cottage was a scene which, had he been there, would have tempted Augustus to put brush to canvas.

The lane outside the cottage was then much quieter with very little traffic. A trip to Fordingbridge with her two young children and Afghan hound would have been a morning's expedition for Juliette. A walk which would have included passing the time of day along the way with her various forester neighbours, and again with the gypsies gathered in the town shopping.

With only one room and small alcove kitchen, living in the cottage was primitive. The water was fetched daily from the well by Juliette and heated on the stove. The gentle pace of life which she lived at the cottage must have been idyllic – tending her bee skeps in the long grass of the garden, planting herbs and flowers, and collecting the wild herbs from the water-meadow to use with oils in her remedies. Then in the evenings with her two children and hound bathing in the cool water of nearby Windsmore pond, she would sometimes return home after dark by the light of a lantern. Juliette did her work after the children had gone to bed, writing her notes about herbs and the Forest until far into the night, often falling asleep before the fire.

಄

Now with the ground floor of the cottage in good repair and clean inside we decided to use it for a studio as both Arthur and I paint. The place seemed to create the right atmosphere with the view of the water-meadow through the tiny rear window and the sounds of wildlife all around. On dark winter evenings there would be strange noises outside which usually proved to be the ponies walking up the lane or perhaps the cattle browsing on the holly hedge. On windy nights there was the constant rustle of the laurel trees.

One evening in May we were painting when there was a knock on the door. To our great surprise we found Juliette had returned to the cottage. She was staying with a friend in the village on a short visit from her home in Galilee.

The weather was particularly bad for the time of year with days of wind and rain but she said she loved it and was enjoying every minute of it. She had just spent a few days in Dorset and had bathed in a mill pond but regretted very much not having time to bathe in Windsmore pond as she loved the cold water.

The lilac tree planted by her beside the cottage when she lived there was in full bloom. It was a beautiful lilac called President Grevy and had now grown to a height of nine feet with the top bent over under the cluster of pale mauve heavily scented blossoms. One of these blossoms we picked for Juliette to press and take back to Galilee with her.

It was very nostalgic for her to be back in the cottage again. That afternoon she had been to visit Gypsy friends, and said how she missed the Gypsies in Galilee but had the Bedouins as her friends instead. Whilst in the cottage Juliette chose one of my paintings of kingcups in the water-meadow to take home with her. Realizing it was rather large and already having a lot of luggage she decided to leave it until she came again.

We talked of friends she knew during her stay in the Forest. I was able to tell her that the talented Juanita who now lived in our village and had at one time been married to painter and sculptor Sven Berlin had recently had a book of poems published. In a television programme she was shown driving along the lanes in a pony and trap whilst her poems were being read.

Juanita was herself a colourful person, always dressed in bright floral skirts down to her ankles. Her dark hair was long, and she wore big golden ear-rings. As well as writing she also painted, especially horses. Her artistic talents did not stop there as she decorated the eaves of her bungalow with large flowers painted in various colours.

Juliette was also interested to hear about Sven Berlin's exhibition of paintings and sculpture which was held in his forest studio at Minstead. When we visited the exhibition he was working on a big sculpture of Madonna and Child which was a special commission. We found it very impressive. A painting which I thought portrayed the Forest in winter stood about three feet high and was a palette knife rendering of one of the giant Redwood trees being lashed with rain.

It was a while before we saw Juliette again but when she did return it was on Christmas Day and she brought her daughter Luz with her. Unfortunately it was only a flying visit as she was on her way to London but she did stay long enough to drink a glass of marrow brandy which we had made from a recipe in her forest book.

ଓ

After a year of painting at every possible moment I eventually accumulated sufficient paintings to hold an exhibition in the cottage. My subject was of course the wild life of the surrounding forest flowers, birds and animals – and Romany life. The walls of the cottage were covered with paintings.

Long-ear and tawny owls peered down from the corners of the room whilst a spotlight illuminated a gypsy van pulled by two horses lumbering up the hill to Abbots Well. On the opening evening of the exhibition the cottage came alive with people coming and going, and lights blazed from the windows. It was August and during the day the temperature had reached well into the eighties which left the evening balmy and airless. We had a small marquee on the grass beside the cottage where the viewers could refresh themselves with a glass of wine. The exhibition lasted for a month with many visitors making it a great success.

On another occasion I was surprised and equally delighted to see a Gypsy bow-top van pull into our gateway from the lane. It was Peter Terson, the playwright, with his lovely old horse Clarence pulling the van. He had just finished filming the television series of his journey from Romsey to the Chalke Valley, and was on another trek now with his friend and dog. They left Clarence tethered outside whilst they came in to see the cottage.

A short time after this visit we met Peter leading the old horse down the hill from Abbots Well. He had walked him across the forest along Hampton Ridge on his way to retirement in field with another horse at the Blissford home of Malcolm and Christopher Horsburgh. For quite a few years Clarence grazed happily with his companions and on occasions would pull a cart around the village for exercise.

The garden that we planted around the cottage after clearing away all the brambles and cutting back the laurels was now beginning to grow. The quince tree in its first year bore two lovely pear-shaped fruit, the moss rose had a shower of pink flowers, and the honeysuckle was halfway up the trellis beside the cottage door. But it would be another season before it became truly established.

CG

3 The Garden by the Well

DURING OUR FIRST YEAR AT Abbots Well – apart from clearing away the brambles, clipping hedges, and cutting grass – we left the garden as it was to see which plants and shrubs were growing there. It was a wild garden being constantly invaded on all sides by the forest, not only the vegetation but also, thankfully, by the birds and wild creatures .

In spring the garden was alive with the dancing wings of brimstone butterflies, their colour competing with that of the wild daffodils which grew in clumps in the grass, and the paler primroses under the hedges. Later in the year, when the Michaelmas daisies were in bloom, the brilliant Red Admiral and equally colourful Peacock butterflies spent the mellow days of autumn on these flowers in the herbaceous border. The bees from the hives in the meadow below the garden spent their summer collecting the nectar from the flowers and, later, the pollen from the autumn flowering ivy for their winter stores.

The birds differed from those visiting my former Wiltshire garden, where starlings and sparrows together with tits and robins were the main inhabitants. In the Forest garden there were wood warblers and nuthatches, greenfinches and longtail tits, and, in winter feeding on the holly berries, redwings and fieldfares. It was delightful to be awakened in the morning by the gentle cooing of wood pigeons or in spring by the wild call of curlews across the forest and sometimes the cuckoo on the apple tree below the window. Then after sunset the soft whirring of nightjars could be heard from their furzy hideaway .

Some of the birds were resident whilst others were just passing through. Once a redstart spent the morning sitting in the apple tree. A pair of spotted flycatchers returned every year to the same little nest-box on the side of the cottage to raise a family.

One of the most amusing birds was a nuthatch that came to and fro to the bird-table for bread, hiding it in various places. It pushed pieces under loose bark on the trees, between the lattice fence, down the sides of two stone pots, and in numerous other places.

Then there was the family of great green woodpeckers, five in all, ungainly looking as they played on the lawn and noisy too. We also had visits from a lesser spotted woodpecker which had a bad leg and could not pitch on the side of the trees but it adapted accordingly and sat on the lawn eating bread.

Amongst our favourite resident birds of the garden was the mysterious tawny owl which lived in the ivy-clad tree that stood outside the landing window. This ancient tree was choked with clusters of ivy hiding many old pigeons' nests in its thick branches. Often, at the end of the day, the owl would sit on one of the boughs, occasionally turning its head to look around, but was most graceful at dusk silently gliding through the branches or sitting high in the birches silhouetted against a pale sky.

Apart from the wild birds we introduced white fantail pigeons to the garden. It really happened quite by accident. Walking along the beach one day we came across a barrel that had been washed in by the tide. This we thought would make a wonderful dovecot. So by carrying and rolling it Arthur managed to get it along the beach, across a field, and into the boot of the car. After several soakings with fresh water to rid it of salt the barrel was left to dry out thoroughly. Arthur then cut off the top, shaped the entrances, and painted it white. Our local thatcher put a roof on and it was then erected in the garden.

A friend gave us a pair of young pigeons only just able to fly. We collected them one evening in a large basket, and on returning home wired them into the cote. After a week the wire was removed and they were given their freedom. Although the pigeons stayed in the garden they did not return to the cote but made their home on top of the oil tank where they eventually nested and layed one egg.

We were surprised one morning to see a strange pigeon come out of the dovecot. It was a large cock-bird which stayed for several days, thoroughly upsetting our own pair. He went away for a while but was soon back again to take possession of the garden. We were even more surprised a fortnight later to see three pigeons in the cote. The first stranger was at the top and two new arrivals below. Most of the day was spent fighting for the top compartment. They were still squabbling when we went out but, on returning home in the evening, we found the stranger in sole possession and that the other two had gone to roost elsewhere.

Yet another pigeon arrived to make four strangers altogether. After three weeks we decided something had to be done as they were upsetting our own pair and pecking the baby. One by one we caught the intruders and gave them to a man who kept pigeons in a loft. So once again peace reigned in the garden, or at least so we thought. But to our dismay the squab of our own pair vanished, it was only just able to fly so it could not have gone very far. We searched everywhere and eventually came to the sad conclusion that a hawk must have taken it.

Two days later I was working quietly in the kitchen when I thought I heard a faint fluttering coming from the back of the boiler. I listened but heard nothing more. When Arthur came home he opened the trap door into the boiler chimney and placed a mirror inside to look up. There, half-way up on a protruding brick, was the baby pigeon. Unfortunately it was just out of arm's reach but using a stick with a loop of wire on the top Arthur managed to topple the baby pigeon off the brick, catch hold the end of its wing and gently pull it down. When the bird came out of the chimney it was black and its eyes full of soot, but with careful bathing the poor creature was soon able to open them. We tried washing the pigeon all over but it turned a dark grey and remained so for many weeks. The parents took a few hours before they recognized and fed their offspring.

ଓଃ

One handsome but mischievous resident in the garden was squirrel. Its drey was at the top of a yew tree in the wood beyond the cottage. With great agility it leapt from branch to branch; on the ground, with skipping hops across the lawn it resembled thistledown blown by the breeze. At first squirrel was very timid but one morning whilst we were having breakfast it appeared on the verandah and as every movement of ours was visible, we had to keep quite still which resulted in cold tea and bacon. But we were rewarded as squirrel had not long taken a perch on top of the stone flower-pot when its mate arrived. They took all the bread put out for the birds and finished by helping themselves to an apple from the tree before vanishing into the depths of the oak tree.

Gradually squirrel became tamer and would wait by the open French window for bread to be put out, and eventually it fed from my hand.

In autumn the squirrels would gather nuts and acorns from the trees and bury them all over the garden. The amazing thing was they knew exactly where to find the nuts again in the winter. I think the secret is that they peel off the husks and puncture each individual nut with their sharp little teeth before burying them and this enables the squirrels to locate the nuts again by smell.

Often squirrels will strip the bark from a tree for the same reason as badger does - for the sugar in the inner layer; also the bark is used to line their dreys. They can do quite a lot of damage in this manner.

One of the garden squirrels developed a taste for the young shoots of the medlar, whilst another took all the half-grown apples from the Beauty of Bath tree. A more expensive piece of damage happened when a pair decided to penetrate the thatch of the cottage through a rusty hole in the wire. A small price to pay though for the pleasure gained from close glimpses of the squirrels private life, suckling their young on the garden seat, or carrying them in their mouth one by one across the garden to a new location.

One day we had great fun watching when squirrel arrived accompanied by two babies; they played games up and down the trees, chased away the birds on the lawn, including the pigeons, then picked the young apples that were just setting. Afterwards they were frequent visitors to the garden mainly to take bread from the bird table, often staying to play. They would stand on their hind legs and box in the same way as a hare does or roll over and over in one big furry ball. But their favourite game was chasing the birds. One morning a fine rook with his feathers all shining in the sunlight descended on the lawn and at once one of the young squirrels chased after him and almost caught him by the tail feathers. The highlight in the lives of the garden squirrels was the arrival of the corn hopper put down for the fantail pigeons. The bird bread was now ignored as they spent their time munching corn.

Squirrels are unpopular with the wild birds as they are great robbers of nests. I remember an incident between a squirrel and a pair of crows in the meadow beside the garden. My attention was drawn by a commotion; deciding to investigate I arrived in time to see a squirrel rolled into a ball falling through the air from about nine feet. Two crows attacked the creature as it reached the ground and it ran for the shelter of the hedge. My impression was that the crows caught the squirrel either in or near their nests and one of them picked it up and dropped it to the ground.

The starlings grew tired of having their nest box, which was attached to the oak tree facing the house, raided every spring so they eventually abandoned it. After the starlings vacated the box squirrel took it over as a lookout and would sit with just head and front paws protruding from the hole and, on occasions, fell fast asleep.

One day a much more wicked looking face was peering out of the starling box. When the animal emerged it proved to be a stoat; obviously doing the same as squirrel – looking for birds' nests. It searched amongst the ivy on the tree before returning to the ground where it spent some time weaving in and out of the hedge before crossing the lawn and climbing the bank out on to the forest. A few days later the stoat was back in the garden again causing a disturbance amongst the birds. They were all gathered around a low ivy-covered tree stump – blackbirds, tits, sparrows, and finches, each one shrieking out its own particular alarm call. I was just in time to see the stoat vanish into the depths of the hedge. I suddenly realized that there was a nest of young robins almost ready to fly in the tree stump and raced to the rescue. On investigation I found that the fledglings had gone and the nest had been pulled to pieces which accounted for the agitation of all the other garden birds. Sadly I went back indoors and one by one the birds dispersed and returned to normal. Later that day I noticed a pair of robins flying in and out of the garden carrying food from the bird table. The next morning I was delighted to see a family of young robins flying around the lawn having pieces of worm thrust down their throats. So the robins managed to save their babies after all. It was probably because they were ready to leave the nest and must have tumbled in all directions when the stoat attacked.

The garden birds have to be constantly on their guard as they have many predators. The hedge-hopping sparrow-hawk that comes gliding through the garden accounts for birds. Sometimes not only the small birds are victims as we discovered one crisp winter afternoon just as the light was fading. We had been brushing leaves and burning them at the bottom of the orchard, and were just raking out the last embers when there was a screech from a bird overhead in the oak tree. Looking up we were just in time to see a hawk with a redwing in its talons fly from the tree down to the boggy ground outside the hedge. No sooner had it landed than it took off again, still clutching the redwing, only to land on the bank across the lane. We ran to the spot where the hawk had landed but, as darkness was falling, we were unable to find any trace of hawk or redwing.

ର

Rabbits often came onto the lawn. Although the garden was fairly well wired they always managed to squeeze in somewhere. Most destructive were the baby rabbits as they would hide in the herbaceous border and nibble the young plants. One spring we lost all our crocuses, there was a patch of them in full bloom and one rabbit accounted for them all, we caught it in the act. The funniest thing was to see a rabbit sitting up with a long green moustache; it was a doe holding a bunch of grass in her mouth which she was gathering to make a nest. For half the morning she was coming and going snatching off the grass and carrying it down the bank and into a hole.

Sitting on the lawn one morning was a jet black rabbit. Not quite believing our eyes we went out into the garden and tried to approach it. Judging by its size and colour the rabbit was obviously domestic but where it had come from we could not imagine. That morning was the beginning of a long frustrating week for although the rabbit was tame it was determined not to be caught. After trying to burrow under the cottage – leaving a big hole and the flowers devastated it dug itself into the most inaccessible places, knowing that they would be out of our reach. In the end Arthur made a box with a sliding door and lengthy piece of string attached. He baited the trap with lettuce and then prepared himself for a long wait, hiding behind a tree whilst holding the other end of the string. Eventually black rabbit followed the trail of lettuce into the box; Arthur let go of the string and the sliding door came down with a bang and our unwelcome visitor was caught at last. Despite squeals when being lifted from the box it soon succumbed to the calming effect of gentle stroking. During the week we had made extensive enquiries to see if anyone had lost a pet. Our local policeman told us of a garden in the neighbouring village that was full of tame rabbits both black and white. So, as soon as black rabbit had calmed down, Arthur took it to join its friends but how it came to be in our garden half-a mile away we shall never know.

I think perhaps our largest uninvited guest was Len's cow Dolly. Every year she had a calf which often she would ignore leaving it asleep on the forest under a bush. But when the time came for her calf to be taken away the cow really made a fuss. On this occasion Len put Dolly into the meadow beside the house the day that her calf had been sent to market. All day she wandered around the field mooing and bellowing, but during the evening the mooing became distinctly louder until one bellow was so close it could have been in the room. Drawing back the verandah curtains we came face to face with Dolly looking in the window. She had forced the wire fence and must have done a spectacular leap to get into the garden as there is a three foot drop into the field. Nevertheless, being dark she had come straight to the light of the window, and no damage was done to plants or flowers.

㴈

Foxes came after dark to the garden. This we knew by the eerie howl under the bedroom window, quite spine-chilling if you are not familiar with their call.

Quite the most horrific happening in the garden took place one morning halfway through breakfast. One minute the birds were singing peacefully, and the next all hell was let loose. A fox burst into the garden through a hole in the fence followed by a pack of hounds. Seeking refuge, it tried to climb the apple tree beside the window whereupon it was grabbed by the jaws of the ferocious dogs. Each took a bite at the poor creature and tore it to pieces. Huntsmen on foot invaded the garden picking up the hounds and throwing them over the hedge into the lane, the master shouting something about the fox having killed thirty chicken the night before. This I learned afterwards was his standard excuse. But during the whole sickening episode there was never a word of apology from master or hunt servants, neither did they clean up the mess. It took Arthur an hour to clean up the bits of bloody fur and entrails and hose down the lawn. I wonder how many of the dressed up followers have actually witnessed this spectacle at close hand; usually they are sitting on their horses half a mile away from the kill.

CB

To return to more pleasant things – though perhaps to some people adders are unpleasant. When we moved to the forest we fully expected frequently to find snakes in the garden, but during our first year we only saw one. One Sunday morning Arthur was about to get under the caravan to do a repair when he noticed an adder curled up in the grass quite close to him. He fetched a broom whilst I got the camera; gently brushing the reptile out into the daylight we were able to photograph it. The snake was, unusually, dark chocolate-brown, though it had the normal markings. Afterwards with the help of another broom we were able to transport the adder out of the garden and release it into the Forest. Although we do not see many snakes in the garden it is a drill with us in summer that, before weeding the borders or lifting any heaps of garden refuse or even walking in long grass, we probe it first. This applies to walking off the tracks in the Forest; it is not advisable to wear open sandals, and a walking stick is a good idea to thump heavily as you walk the vibrations will alert any sleeping snake which will then slip away quietly.

CB

The first spring and summer brought forth many flowers and shrubs already growing in the garden so we were able to plan around them. There was of course the mauve President Grevy lilac which Juliette planted and also a white one beside the gate. The philadelphus was covered in blossom; this to me is a wedding flower, and beneath it was a carpet of lily-of-the-valley. Red hot pokers smouldered at the back of the border, one of which was adopted by the robin as his favourite perch and lookout. Perhaps the most colourful were the polyanthus which lined the borders at the front and sides of the house in spring, and later in summer there were Florabunda roses, Masquerade and Moulin Rouge.

Under the kitchen window was a rosemary bush and beside it I planted a southernwood which came from my Wiltshire garden. This artemisia herb is a particular favourite of mine; I hang small bunches of it in the clothes and linen cupboards. Its pungent smell resembling a mild disinfectant it helps to deter moths, together with tablets of sharp smelling soap.

The summer had produced a large crop of apples on the four old trees in the garden. There was Gascoyne's Scarlet – a crisp juicy apple, whose fruit when ripe glows like lanterns from the foliage. Another tree was so old that even when Juliette sent samples of the leaves and fruit to experts they were unable to identify it. She renamed it Tawny Gypsy, its golden skin being reminiscent of the suntanned gypsies. A smaller tree was a very old russet and another the versatile Newton Wonder which can be used as a dessert or cooker.

The boughs of the Tawny Gypsy tree were heavy with fruit; one branch was almost bent to the ground and needed to be supported by a prop. The young blue and great tits which hatched in spring were still resident in the garden and took delight in flying from tree to tree, pecking every apple they came upon.

But the blackbird sat firmly beside one apple until it had almost hollowed out the inside. If the apples were left very much longer on the tree the whole crop would have been ruined, so we decided to gather them in the following weekend.

The apple store had to be tidied up and one side cleared and fitted with a series of racks down the wall on which to store the apples. The following Saturday and Sunday was spent up and down the ladder, and to and fro to the cottage with baskets laden with fruit. The handle of my favourite basket became weakened under the weight. The apples were separated into various grades – good for keeping, the bruised for cooking and wine making – then spread on sheets of paper on the floor. Several evenings were spent transporting them from the cottage to the apple store. Without electricity in the store, everything had to be done by moonlight and the dim light of an oil lantern. The blended smell of apples and burning oil is something I shall connect with crisp autumn evenings for a long time.

The winter brought snow to our Abbots Well garden, making it spectacular with laden branches and hedge tops. It was interesting to see which animals had visited the garden during the night by the prints and trails they left in the snow. The birds became extra hungry; the robins, forgetting their territorial fights all fed together on the bird-table, sometimes as many as six at one time.

Beautiful as all this was we were impatient for the spring to see the results of the many bulbs, shrubs, and trees, we had planted. During an autumn visit to Cornwall we filled a sack with daffodil bulbs which had been discarded by a market garden on waste ground near Penzance. They were in perfect condition and we planted them in the grass beneath the apple trees, and under the hedges to add to those already there. A neighbour gave me three peony roots which came from her mother's forest garden at Ogdens. One was a double red, another was a scented pink, and the third was a big single white with a yellow centre, also with a delicate perfume. As peonies do not like to be disturbed it would probably be two or three years before they bloomed.

Azalea and rhododendron cuttings had also been planted. Some of these were brought from a beautiful forest garden at Minstead. The owner gave them to my husband when he left his flat in the big house to get married. Others, including a bright orange azalea, came from Exbury Gardens. These lovely gardens, which stretch down to the Beaulieu River, are open to the public in springtime when the azaleas and rhododendrons are a blaze of colour, then again at the end of the year for the autumn tints.

We planted two very old types of trees near to the cottage – a quince and medlar – but it would be several years before they were at their best. The exotic fruit of the quince is lime yellow in colour and has a sharp smell with a slight resemblance to gardenias. It has a dual purpose as it makes a very palatable jelly to serve with cold meat. Also one or two fresh picked fruit placed in a dish will give a pleasant fragrance to a room. The medlar fruit makes a jelly reminiscent in taste of Canadian maple syrup; after being picked the medlars have to be left to ripen until they appear rotten. To eat them raw in this way is, I think, an acquired taste. The foliage of the medlar tree in autumn is spectacular, turning through reds and oranges to gold.

During the first winter we decided to establish bees once again in the garden, but not for at least two years as we knew nothing about them and would have to take some training. Arthur attended evening classes at agricultural college the following winter and in the meantime read all the books he could find on the subject becoming fascinated by it. We looked forward to our first hive.

4 Bees and Honey

BY THE FOLLOWING SPRING THE garden was well established. The rhododendrons and azalea cuttings brought from another forest garden were growing well and the hedge behind the awaiting hive was entwined with honeysuckle and bramble flowers.

The nucleus of bees complete with queen duly arrived and was installed in the hive. The bees were a light golden brown in colour and of a docile strain. They settled in quickly and were soon back and forth from the hive to the meadow. There they had a choice of many wild flowers and herbs such as ragged robin, water flags, kingcups, clover and numerous others. Later in the summer they had at their disposal the wide expanses of heather just over the hedge beyond the garden. The laurel trees around the cottage also provided the bees with nectar, which they found on the undersides of the leaves. The sunshine has a part to play in the honey flow, for without the warmth that only the sun can provide the flowers will not give up their nectar. Some flowers require more heat than others; for example, bramble blossom needs only a little, whereas clover requires a great deal.

Keeping a few hives has always been a Forest tradition, probably due to the continuous flow of nectar from the early oak blossom to the late blooming heather. One of the bees' greatest sources of pollen was from the acres of gorse just over the hedge on the open forest. Unable to reach the nectar due to the tightly sealed blossoms, the bees gathered the pollen from this aromatic bush for their winter stores. Nectar supplies the bees with protein and pollen with carbohydrates.

Our new hive was square in shape and constructed from cedar wood. Arthur made it himself during his training session at the Agricultural College.

The original homes of the New Forest bees were straw skeps. These round skeps were made by the gypsies beside their camp fires. A lot of work and skill went into their making; they were woven with twists of straw which were bound around with strings of seasoned bramble. The gypsies gathered long lengths of bramble removed the thorns and cut them into strips. These were then tied in bundles and left to dry. In very early days it is believed bee hives were of a domed pattern, high and peaked, and made of stitched bark or wattled osiers. Before use they were scoured with crushed balm and honeywort.

Colonies of wild bees are to be found in numerous hollow trees in the Forest. They probably originate from swarms leaving hives in the foresters' gardens to seek new homes. Most of these are a strain called New Forest Blacks which are reputed to be very bad-tempered. We came across one such tree – a large, partially hollow oak, on Old Sloden Hill. There were hundreds of bees coming and going; their accumulated stores of honey in the depths of the trunk must have been considerable. The honey itself was pure as the wild bees would have fed on their own stores during the winter instead of the sugar syrup given to bees in domestic hives. Also the honey would contain all the fragrance of the Forest, the nectar having been gathered from the blossoms of the holly and ivy, heather and numerous other flowers without fear of contamination from chemical sprays.

On another occasion whilst searching for pieces of Roman pottery we came upon a fallen tree. The impact of hitting the ground had split the trunk open; fragments of comb had fallen out and lay scattered around. Any honey that had been inside that tree the badgers would have found. They love honey, and seem to disregard the bee stings when attacking a wild beehive. At one time the keepers were entitled to take any wild honey from the Forest, if they were brave enough to collect it.

When Juliette lived in the cottage she had a bee skep, and also a wooden hive in the garden beneath the apple trees. She was horrified when a forester bee-keeper came to take the honey from the skep for her, and said it was customary to drown the bees from Abbots Well garden in the well. She sent him away and left the honey in the skep. Local bee-keeper, Bob Kenchington, also helped Juliette with her bees as he did with ours many years later in our Abbots Well garden.

There is an old saying in the Forest 'A swarm of bees in May is worth a load of hay.' It was May when our bees decided to swarm. The day was warm and sunny, and during the morning the bees had been restless, just flying up and down in front of the hive. Then at noon the buzzing reached a crescendo and a spiral of bees took off from the hive, forming a black mass, and flew off towards the forest. Fortunately the queen followed by the swarm descended on a hawthorn tree beside the wells. As they were fairly low to the ground Arthur was able to collect them quite easily in a straw basket. This he left upside down on the ground with one end raised and resting on a brick so that any stray bees left outside could crawl up inside and join the rest. At dusk he brought the basket of bees complete with queen into the garden. In the meantime an empty hive had been prepared to receive them. We scoured it out with handfuls of mint and lavender, just as we had done the first hive.

In front of the empty hive we placed a board sloping from the ground to the entrance and over this we placed a white sheet. Just as the light was fading Arthur shook the swarm from the basket onto the front of the board. In no time at all hardly any of the white sheet was visible as the mass of bees immediately began to disperse, and like an army on the march walked side by side in an endless line up the covered board back into the hive. But the most amazing part of this episode was the sound, for each bee as it went was buzzing and the combined noise, resounding in the gathering darkness, was quite uncanny.

The two colonies flourished, working ceaselessly when conditions were right and eventually growing so strong that the hives became overcrowded. This meant that once again they swarmed. Unfortunately, both hives did so within a day of each other; we were unable to cope with both in such a short time and had to engage the help of Bob Kenchington. Once again the bees chose the hawthorn tree beside the wells and, as on previous occasions, it happened at midday. This swarm did not settle as quickly as the other and bees were flying to and fro across the lane. We put a BEWARE BEES sign out to warn people as Mr Kenchington and a fellow bee-keeper could not come until the evening. The day had been very hot and sultry and by tea-time dark clouds were gathering and distant rolls of thunder could be heard. It is a well known fact that bees become bad tempered if it is thundery and that evening several stings were acquired. Bob Kenchington was stung on his eye and I received one on my nose whilst showing the whereabouts of the swarm to the bee-keepers. As they began the tedious job of taking the swarm the storm broke with heavy rain, thunder and lightning, but they carried on with their task and eventually all the bees were safely installed inside the nucleus box which was put into the boot of the car to be transported to their new home.

Once again the routine of the two hives reverted to normal as the remaining bees settled down and began working. With regular inspections of the hives everything ran smoothly for the rest of the summer.

○8

When the time came for the removal of the combs they were found to be heavy with honey. For a while these honeycombs were stored in the cottage whilst we were waiting for the extractor. This meant we had to keep the door firmly closed because the bees, smelling the honey, tried hard to get in. Eventually the extractor became available; we were hiring it from the agricultural college and all the necessary equipment was gathered in the bee-house. The bee-house was a wooden construction tucked away on the bank beneath the yew tree. It was twelve by eight feet which meant there was plenty of room inside to work. Being lined with hardboard made it warm and dry, which also helped to keep out the spiders. Either side of the door were hooks for hanging our bee suits and veiled hats. Against the far wall was a large kneehole desk and swivel chair. The drawers of the desk held the literature on bee-keeping; also small tools such as a scraper which was an instrument used for removing from the comb any heather honey that had been mixed with ordinary honey. Standing in the corner were boxes of new jars ready for honey.

We placed the extractor in the centre of the room so as to be able to move around it whilst spinning the honey combs. The combs with their cappings removed are placed in racks inside the drum and spun around by turning a handle. The speed at which they revolve throws the honey out against the sides of the drum. It then runs down the sides and into the bottom of the extractor. When all the honey has been extracted it is transferred to storage tins by means of a tap. It is then left a day or two to settle before bottling off. Cleaning out the drum afterwards is a very sticky job .

Heather honey, being so much thicker than normal honey, cannot be extracted by spinning. The cappings are first removed with a hot knife and the comb containing the honey is scraped off down to the foundation. The heather honey and pieces of wax comb are then placed in a plastic bucket and left to drain. Eventually the honey will run out, leaving the bits of comb which can be used afterwards for making mead. As the combs containing heather honey have been cut away down to the foundations it means the bees have extra work in the spring rebuilding the cells. With ordinary honey the cells are left intact, ready to receive fresh honey when returned to the hive. After extracting the honey from the combs they are put back into the hiverthe bees will clean them up ready to use again.

When we removed our first frames of honey from the hive we

found we had quite a lot of wild comb – pieces of wax made by the bees to fill up gaps that are not the right size. For example, the space between the frames in the hive has to be just large enough for a bee to pass to and fro, otherwise they will wax up the surplus space. We saved all our wild comb and cappings to make our own mead. We did it in much the same way as the forester back in ancient times, using the water from Abbots Well. The water needs to be soft; rainwater is excellent, as it affects the quality of the wax. The water is heated to melt the wax and separate the honey. When it is cold the wax should rise to the top; it can then be lifted off in one piece.

Our recipe for Abbots Well Mead is as follows: Place the cappings and pieces of wild comb in a pan, add enough cold soft water or rainwater to cover, and bring to the boil. Simmer gently until the wax rises to the top. Allow to cool. Remove the wax, strain the remaining liquor into a covered vessel. When luke warm stir in one teaspoonful of mead yeast and put in a warm place to ferment. When bubbling has ceased, strain into a cask with air-lock and store for a year before bottling off.

&#x08;

At one time the New Forest was famed for the mead brewed by the forester. The refuse and the imperfect combs from the skeps were boiled up and the liquor strained of and stored in earthenware pots until it fermented. This very potent brew often led to drunkenness which gave rise to a lighthearted story in the Forest. It is said that if a visitor had been unpleasant during his stay he would be given a large drink of mead before his departure in the hope that he would fall from his pony before reaching home.

Back in Anglo-Saxon times mead was in common use. It was served at royal banquets and at wayside inns alike. Even in the monasteries the monks had an allowence. There were three kinds of mead brewed in those days. One, known as Pigment, was made from pure honey with various spices added and laced with of a type of wine. This was the mead probably served in the manor houses on the occasion of a royal visit. Another, called morat, was a mixture of honey, water and the juice of mulberries, the trees of which flourished all over England at that time. This mead was probably drunk by the lords of the manor and their families. The third was of course the common mead brewed by the forester, using the refuse from his skep.

It was possible that in the year of a good heather crop the forester would have brewed a luxury mead using the pure heather honey. We did this in our second year. The heather that summer was good, with a carpet spread before us over the Forest as far as the eye could see, and the sun shone for days on end supplying the warmth needed for the blossoms to give up their nectar.

And here is a recipe for Sweet Mead: Four pounds of heather honey, one gallon of water, half an ounce of mead yeast. Boil the water and pour over the warmed honey. Leave to cool, when lukewarm add the yeast, and leave in a warm room to ferment. When bubbling has ceased leave to stand in a cool place for a few weeks. Strain into a cask and store for a year before bottling off.

The temptation was great after we had bottled the mead to sample it. But it improves with keeping and should be left to mature for several years. However we did open a bottle after a year and found it quite delightful although some people might find it too sweet especially those who prefer their wine dry.

The honey fortunately did not have to be left to mature and could be eaten immediately. We found we had more than enough honey for ourselves even after leaving supplies in the hives for the bees' winter feeding, so we decided to sell the surplus. We placed a 'Honey for Sale' sign on the gate, and stacked the jars of honey on a shelf in the cottage. We thought whilst people were buying the honey they could also see the cottage where Juliette lived. Although her book was out of print it was still available from libraries, and people were always coming to see the cottage and the wells.

5 Badgers

I<small>T WAS A DARK WINTER'S</small> night when first we discovered badgers were visiting the garden. Whilst having supper at a table by the window overlooking the verandah a movement outside attracted our attention and there, looking out from behind an ornamental flowerpot, was a badger. It quickly vanished but to our delight a few minutes later a large badger stepped out of the shadow into a shaft of light shining from the window, then quickly disappeared again into the darkness.

On the following evening we put scraps of fat bacon and bread and honey onto the verandah and kept vigil until midnight but nothing happened. It was a week before we saw badger again, he then came to the low rustic table on which we put the scraps of food. He ate all that was put out for him despite being illuminated by the light from the house.

After that evening we frequently saw Bill Badger (so we named him) as he came to the verandah table most nights. Arthur thought of a way for Badger to announce himself when entering the garden.

He made a small wooden platform and buried it under the ground by the hole in the fence where badger was coming in. It had contacts beneath it and was wired to a bell in the house so the moment he came through the fence and his feet depressed the platform the bell rang in the house. But not every time was it a badger; on several occasions the bell heralded the arrival of a tabby cat. This system worked very well until one morning we discovered the platform lying on top of the ground where Bill had dug it up. As he fed with his front paws resting on the verandah table we decided to transfer the contacts and wire to beneath the table top. Bill Badger became used to noises and lights from the house and, to a certain extent, human scent.

One evening he was accompanied by a sow but she was timid and stayed in the shadows, venturing gingerly into the light. Badger did quite a lot of digging in the garden; if he scented a mole he dug right down to its run. He was also very fond of tulip bulbs, choosing them in preference to daffodils and hyacinths. All over the lawn there were little holes made by his snout whilst searching for worms.

A badger's diet consists mainly of earth worms, slugs, moles, beetles and other small mammals but, being omnivorous, vegetable matter is also included. A particular treat for a badger is for him to find a wasps' or wild bees' nest. He will dig it out devouring the larvae, adults, comb, and in the case of the latter, the honey.

After seeing badgers in the garden during the winter we thought that now spring was approaching it would be interesting to sit over a sett in the forest and view them in their natural surroundings. The best time for badger watching is early spring, before the bracken grows tall and the midges are about. On warm evenings the cubs come above ground well before sunset to play, often staying after the adults have left for their nightly feeding expeditions.

Not having sat over a sett in the wild before there were numerous things to be taken into consideration before we set out. As we had to get permission from the keeper whose area the sett was in we decided to ask his advice. The following are a few tips he gave us. Clothing should be carefully chosen for as spring progresses the mosquitos and midges increase. Every part of the body needs to be covered with even a net veil over the face. As midges can penetrate through wool, leather gloves are best, and wellies to protect the ankles. Sitting still for two hours or more one soon becomes quite chill even on a warm evening so an extra sweater is advisable. All clothing should be dark in colour and soft so as not to rustle as you move.

On approaching the sett do so by taking a few steps then stopping; repeat this all the way, giving the impression of a grazing animal to the badgers beneath ground who will then be unperturbed. Remember also to keep downwind and the same applies before choosing a place to observe from otherwise the badgers with their keen sense of smell will soon detect you and return down their holes for the rest of the night. An instant indicator you could use is a small bottle-type container of powder. A squeeze will puff the powder into the air and the gentle breeze will carry it away and leave you in no doubt where to position yourself. Be sure you sit against a tree rather than between them as your silhouette will be a new object to the badgers which will immediately put them on their guard. Small folding seats are more comfortable than sitting on the ground as you need to keep very still once the badgers are out. Always arrive in daylight well before sunset as on warm summer evenings the cubs come out to play very early. Also focus your binoculars on the sett in daylight, then, as it becomes dim in the wood and the first badgers appear, you will be ready. Try to avoid frightening the wildlife above ground as an animal or bird alarm call will alert the badgers and postpone their appearance.

⊗

One evening in late April we reached the area of the sett which we had chosen to watch. The woodmen had been busy cutting down fir trees at the entrance of the wood and the air was heavy with the smell of fresh sawn timber. We settled ourselves against a tree downwind from the sett to keep watch. The visibility was good as the bracken had not yet grown and the midges were not about. The wait was by no means boring; sitting quietly you realize how much life there is going on in what seems to be a deserted wood. We had not been there very long when a roe deer passed within feet of us, grazing as it went, not realizing anyone was close by.

The birds were having their last song before going to roost, and the distant cry of a curlew could be heard. Just as dusk was gathering a group of ponies walked right over the sett. We thought that would certainly keep the badgers down, but to our delight one popped its head out of a hole and sniffed the air. Satisfying itself that all was well it came right out, followed by another. For a long time the badgers kept coming and going in and out of the holes until eventually two went off in different directions in search of food. Feeling cold and stiff, and with darkness upon us we thought it time to move. So, by torch light we made our way home. For me it was an exciting evening, although I had seen badgers in our own garden, it was the first time I had actually seen them at their sett.

The next evening we returned again and settling ourselves down we could see a herd of fallow deer in the distance, and the roe we had seen the evening before was grazing not far away. Two wild duck flew overhead, followed not long after by a woodcock grumbling to itself as it went.

It was to prove a fruitful evening with not such a long wait as before. The light was fading fast when an eerie screech of an owl rang out through the trees followed by a hoot somewhere in the distance. At that moment the first badger appeared sniffing the air from inside the hole before coming right out into the open. Quite close to the sett was a herd of cattle, all moving quite fast but grazing as they went, and rustling the leaves underfoot. The badger was quite unperturbed by all this until one of the cows stepped on a stick which cracked like a gunshot. This made brock freeze in its steps for a few moments but, satisfying itself there was no danger, continued on its way. Approaching a pile of dead bracken and leaves it gathered up a bundle in its front paws and shuffled backwards towards its hole dragging it along the ground and eventually backed down the hole with the fresh bedding.

This particular sett was a very large one housing several families.

It was amusing to watch as there were a number of smaller holes scattered around near the larger ones, and badgers kept popping their heads in and out of these, giving the impression of a large Punch and Judy show.

Eventually, as dusk fell the adult badgers left the sett and went their separate ways into the night to hunt for food. It was not long before the cubs came out to play; we counted five all squeaking and rolling beside an old tree stump. We watched until it was too dark to see any more, then reluctantly turned for home, leaving the cubs still playing and romping in the darkness.

A week later we went back to the sett with a camera and flash attachment. The bracken was already standing about four inches high around the sett and ready to uncurl. This would probably be our last chance to try for photographs. I usually sat on a small folding seat with my back against a tree, and Arthur sat on a sack on the ground with two fir branches propped up in front as a hide. That particular evening, having the camera, Arthur decided to stand. Quite soon a nose appeared at one of the entrances and sniffed the air. Being such a still evening there was not enough breeze to carry our scent away and it must have hung in the air as the badger immediately got wind of us and returned down its hole.

We waited an hour and a half, Arthur still standing with the camera poised ready to snap. My stool had tipped at an angle where he had nudged me with his knee every time he thought he saw a badger, one more nudge would have tipped me right over completely spoiling our chance. But just as it was almost too dark to see a large badger emerged a few feet away from us. Arthur clicked the camera. I prepared for a blinding flash but nothing happened, in his excitement he got the strap twisted around the camera. Fortunately badger had not heard anything so Arthur was able to take two shots as it was quite unperturbed by the flash. Being satisfied with these two photographs for that evening we crept quietly away and left the badgers in peace.

Back in the garden Badger was still visiting the table, and we could be fairly certain of seeing him early on wet nights, probably because of the darkness. One particularly bad night proved to be no exception when a gale was blowing and rain lashed against the windows. Not thinking of badgers, as I walked from one room to another, I turned on the verandah light and revealed badger half way through a soggy piece of bread and honey. Its coat was sparkling with raindrops and sticking out in wet spikes showing all the pale fur beneath.

I watched Badger using his paws gracefully to drag the food from the table, or sometimes standing on his hind legs with both front paws on the table. Before finishing his supper a noise in the lane bothered him and he was gone into the darkness. Sometimes if disturbed badger would come back later in the night, but this time he did not, and the remaining food was still there in the morning.

A few evenings later Bill Badger had his supper against the glow of a heath fire - as he arrived on the verandah to inspect the table a flicker appeared on the hill beyond the garden, and within seconds the wind whipped up great tongues of flame through the furze, but Badger with the tips of his coat lit with gold, continued his meal of bread and honey quite unperturbed.

It was now well into May and we thought for a change we would watch a different sett. There was a large dig we had often seen during daylight walks in the Forest, so we decided to watch this one. We started out much earlier than on previous occasions; being new territory we wanted to take our position in good time, in case the badgers were early risers. It was a beautiful evening; the sun was still quite high and as we entered the enclosure the birds were in full chorus. There was hardly any breeze which meant the fragrance of the forest blossoms hung heavily on the air – the coconut scent of the gorse and the resinous smell of the pines.

We eventually left the path and made our way down through the bluebells on the south-facing slope to where the badgers' holes were situated. There were three well used areas with freshly dug sand at the entrances. We took up our positions on the side of the slope with the sett below us so as to have a clear view, making sure first that we were down wind from the badgers. We then sat with our backs to a tree and quietly waited.

The new, fresh green leaves formed a mantle over our heads but not thick enough to cover completely the blue sky. Through the trees in a distant clearing the ponies were quietly grazing, only a recently born foal found the energy to dart around in a big circle stopping suddenly to nuzzle its mother, then taking off again to complete the circle in the opposite direction. Whilst this was going on a thrush and blackbird were singing somewhere high in the leafy branches. The chiff chaff that had accompanied us along the forest track had now given way to the cuckoo. Suddenly this peaceful scene was shattered by the strident drumming of a woodpecker. A short silence followed - then, one by one, the song birds started up their evening chorus, only to be silenced after a few minutes by the same harsh noise.

As dusk began to fall three people walked along the path above us complete with flash cameras and sound equipment. They frightened a roe deer which came crashing along just behind us, stopping quite close by. Catching sight of our silhouettes it was bewildered by the appearance of a new object in its territory. By this time the light was growing dim and curiosity was getting the better of it. Lifting one leg it stood looking quizzically in our direction, then bent low and peered with its neck outstretched. Suddenly it was away, possibly frightened by a slight movement of ours.

The three people situated themselves on the track about a hundred yards from us immediately upwind of the badger sett, which dispelled any hope of seeing badgers that evening. Nevertheless we decided to sit for a while longer as it was such a lovely evening with so much other wildlife around.

When the last cuckoo faded into the distance a woodcock flew over croaking as it went on its ritual twilight circle of the woods. Once or twice we heard the whirr of a nightjar, obviously the subject of the sound equipment carried by the people. We did not visit the setts again that summer as the badgers back in our garden were now coming earlier as the evenings grew darker.

One cloudless evening the harvest moon rose large and yellow over Hampton Ridge and shone through the leaves of the oak tree at the bottom of the garden. By mid-evening it was high in the sky and the garden was bathed in a silver light; Bill Badger paid an unusually early visit to the table. We had put out bread and bacon fat, so were able to watch him eat it by the light of the moon. He stayed about twenty minutes, and after taking a walk around the garden left. Once again we put out food on the table, and within half an hour the bel rang and there was another badger - this time a smaller one, probably the sow. This was contrary to all the theories of badgers not liking moonlit nights. It is said that they dislike bright moonlight and also wet weather, when they tend to emerge much later, but the badgers that visit the garden seem to delight in wet nights and are always about much earlier.

We discovered that the sett of the badgers which visited the garden was only a quarter of a mile from the house, being situated on high ground in a small sloping wood overlooking the valley. This wood was on private land and the owners had built a hide in a tree immediately over the holes. A friend who watched regularly took us with him one August evening. We arrived just before dusk, rather late I felt. The vibrations of us walking over the sett probably kept them down as we sat in the tree above the sett an hour before anything happened.

Various sounds drifted up from the valley - distant human voices, the grunting and squealing of pigs and, overhead, the clap-clap of wood-pigeons' wings. It was quite dark before the first nose appeared, then three badgers emerged, but all that could be seen were three dark forms running around under the tree. As it was a very dark night without a moon, we decided to leave.

ভ

On a few occasions I have seen badgers out in broad daylight. One afternoon, in the deep forest I surprised one foraging amongst the leaves, but on detecting my scent it was gone. Another time whilst on a walk to see the foxgloves one damp murky afternoon I saw a badger briefly as it crossed my path. I wondered if perhaps there was a sett nearby so I tried to follow its tracks through the bracken, but everything was dripping wet after a morning of heavy thunderstorms.

There were so many tracks leading off in different directions that by following various ones I covered a large part of this particular enclosure. It was one of the very old areas of the Forest, with the ground here and there falling away into gentle valleys, singing with the sound of water gurgling over the stones in deeply gullied brooks now full after the recent heavy rain. The banks of these brooks were thick with moss and hanging ferns, and at intervals there were tracks of mud leading down to the water where the animals came to drink. It was here I saw badger pad prints easy to distinguish by the five claws. The bracken was shoulder-high and all around there were foxgloves giving great splashes of purple to the otherwise green Forest. At one place I came upon a smell resembling that of a dead animal, but upon investigation I found two stinkhorns; a type of fungus cream in colour and giving off an obnoxious odour.

I penetrated deeper into the forest, passing on my way a group of yew trees, one of which was so large in girth that it must have been hundreds of years old. The only animal life I came upon that afternoon was a roe deer which stood looking at me for some seconds before crashing off into the undergrowth. Although I searched for an hour, and found many signs of the presence of badgers, such as bark stripped from the base of the tree trunks, and holes in the soft ground where they had dug their noses in, I could not find the sett. So I gathered a few foxgloves and returned home damp and weary.

ය

One night at the end of summer we were disturbed by terrifying screams coming from the garden. Looking out of the window we could just see the shadowy forms of two badgers fighting on the lawn. Just as suddenly as it had started it stopped and the badgers vanished into the night. For many weeks after that Bill Badger's food was still on the table at dawn, providing a tasty breakfast for the early rising magpies. This was probably because during the autumn the badgers have an abundance of natural food in the Forest, with beech-mast, acorns, and chestnuts, so they have no need to seek scraps from gardens.

As autumn merged into winter the food started to vanish regularly from the table, and there were digs all over the lawn, which was a sure sign that Badger was visiting the garden again. But his calls must have been in the early hours of the morning as we often watched for him until after midnight without success. Then, one evening in December, we were delighted to see Bill Badger's familiar bristly back as he sat on the verandah nibbling meat from a bone. We had hoped that as cub time drew near he would start coming earlier again and now our patience had been rewarded.

The first snow of winter fell and a week later it still lay thick upon the ground, with temperatures below freezing all day. New Year's Eve arrived and still it was a white world. Ice was already forming on the roads when we set out during the evening to go to a party. Before leaving we put the usual food on the table for Badger. When we returned at two o'clock in the morning and came over the brow of the hill the car headlights lit up a dark object in the road. To our horror there was poor Bill Badger lying dead outside our gate. It was a sad sight for he had obviously been hit by a car and was bleeding from the nose.

This was indeed an unhappy start to the New Year. Our only hope now was that perhaps the sow which occasionally came with him to the garden would find a new mate and introduce him to the table.

╋

6 The Surrounding Forest 1

SOON AFTER MOVING TO ABBOTS Well I was tempted by a glorious morning to walk across the forest to the hill above Windsmore pond where I stood for some moments just looking and listening. The sun was glinting on the water of the pond as it was stirred by the breeze; from the marshes in the valley came the ripple of redshanks, and overhead the sharp cry of plovers filled the air as they swooped and circled over the open heathland of Latchmore Bottom. Standing on the hill that morning I realized just how much there was to explore – the Forest around Abbots Well offered great variety. There was open moorland with large stretches of furze and heather where many species of birds were to be seen and which gave cover to several foxes' earths. There were wooded enclosures where badgers had their setts and deer grazed peacefully beneath the shade of the leafy branches. Peat-stained streams meandered their way through wooded glades and open moorland, here and there opening out to deep pools where small brown trout would lie. Treacherous bogs were numerous, deceptive in their beauty with bright green moss, colourful flowers and rushes.

To explore the surrounding Forest there was a lot of ground to cover so we decided that bicycles would be a good form of transport with which to do this. We could then very quickly cover the mile or so of furzy country along the top of Hampton Ridge to reach the beautiful wooded glades of Amberwood and Island Thorns. So on bicycles one morning we made our way to the enclosures. On reaching Islands Thorns we hid our bicycles in the bracken and walked into the woods. Not along the tracks but through the waist high bracken, and into the woods that only a few weeks ago were carpeted with bluebells; now they were guarded by regiments of tall foxgloves nodding and bobbing in shafts of sunlight.

On entering the wood one could feel the atmosphere of great antiquity for all around there were tall trees, mostly oaks, some in various states of decay; in places, where a hollow stump was still standing, ferns and foxgloves were growing out of the top. Fallen trunks were rotting on the ground purposely left for the Forest insects such as beetles, ants, woodlice and many others.

How cool it was beneath the canopy of leafy branches, the air being refreshed by the transpiration from the trees. The trees by way of their roots take in moisture and this sap flows upwards to the leaves. The unwanted water is then discarded by the leaves in the form of vapour, thus cooling the air to beyond the edges of the wood.

The vegetation on the rides was noticeably more lush and the branches of the trees in places were almost touching the ground. The reason for this is that the ponies and cattle are kept out of the woods by the fences surrounding them. The enclosures are then grazed only by the deer who can easily leap the fences.

Fragile honeysuckle was clinging to the tops of the low bushes pale and delicate compared to the blooms on the hedges out in the sunlight. Most noticeable though was the tranquillity within the wood, the subdued light broken only by an occasional shaft of sunlight. Walking along the grassy rides between the columns of giant trees gave one the feeling of wandering down the aisle of a vast, natural cathedral.

We reached a thick fir plantation where the young trees had not had their lower branches trimmed so that, in places, the vegetation was quite dense. We took to the drainage ditch, this being the easiest way to penetrate this section of the Forest. Judging by the numerous tracks in the dried mud, it was apparently the way the animals chose. In one particular spot we disturbed a great green woodpecker feeding beside a giant ant-hill. On closer inspection the mound was found to be alive with a seething mass of ants. It was constructed with bits of twig and thousands of fir needles all collected from the Forest floor by these busy little workers. Being conical in shape and standing at about five feet high these mounds are numerous in the Forest where fir trees flourish and the surrounding ground is soft and spongy. We did not linger very long as the foraging ants, which were huge compared to our garden ones, were swarming all over the ground and crawling on to our shoes, and I felt sure they had a nasty bite.

As we emerged from the gloom of the firs into the light of the oak woods we disturbed a fallow deer which had been sitting on the edge of the plantation. Coming upon a group of young beeches we noticed that several of the smaller trees had their bark stripped away from their roots. This we thought might be an indication that there was a badger sett close by as badgers are said to do this because of the sweetness of the bark in early summer. We came upon several rabbit burrows but nothing resembling a badger sett.

With so much to see and discover the time had passed very quickly so reluctantly we made our way back to the bicycles with a promise to explore further as soon as possible.

ભ

Abbots Well, being situated as it is with miles of open Forest before it, our garden was naturally visited by numerous wild creatures. Many we saw but others just remained weird cries in the night. Although there were deer close by in Hasley and Sloden it was not often that we were able to see them in the open near the house. But one summer afternoon, after a heavy thunderstorm with the forest still damp and steaming, three fallow deer could be seen from the window standing on Windmill Hill. They had probably been frightened out of the enclosures into the open by the terrific crashes of thunder. When it thunders at Abbots Well it rumbles and echoes in the valleys, and rolls from hill to hill.

On another occasion, this time in the morning, we saw a fox running down over Windmill Hill, its coat shining in the sunlight; leaping over the furze it vanished into the thicket at the bottom of the hill. With the promise of a beautiful day we decided to look in the undergrowth to see if there was an earth near at hand as often at night foxes could be heard calling. After searching for an hour amongst the waist-high bracken and furze, we found no sign of an earth.

By now it was getting warm and we had to look carefully where we were treading as this was the kind of place adders were likely to be. All around was the sound of gorse pods popping in the heat and the air was heavy with the scent of honeysuckle that was clinging to the top of every other bush. Eventually we left the thicket and came out onto Hampton Ridge. We then made our way down through the heather to Latchmore Bottom where we took to the stream and waded. It was cool and refreshing though the water was stained brown from the peat.

There was a variety of flowers on the banks of the stream – pale violets and stunted foxgloves, bluebells in the shadier places, and forget-me-nots at the water's edge. We stopped for a while to rest on the cool grassy bank. Everywhere there were dragonflies darting and hovering over the water. Referred to as the dandy of the insect world they are also sometimes called 'horse stinger'. This is because the claspers of the male is mistaken for a stinger, but they are harmless and are only for carrying off the female in the breeding season.

In the morning there had been a large group of horses and cattle congregated on the open green. They had been trying to escape the flies but now, as the breeze stirred, they were beginning to move off. We thought it time to continue on our way also. We followed the stream as closely as possible but in places the alder trees and blackthorn bushes were overhanging the water, making it necessary to walk around them. Beneath these bushes the banks were steeper, and deep dark pools had formed. Most of Latchmore Brook trickled between grassy banks grazed short by the animals. In some places, in contrast to the pools, the gravel bed lay dry and exposed. It was in the deeper water that the little brown trout would lurk, only to dart under cover of the bank when anyone approached. Quite often as the stream dries out in summer the trout are left stranded in these pools until the rains come again. I have seen a shoal of lamprey, in spawning time, as far upstream as Alderhill and sometimes a small pike will find its way having left the Avon by one of its tributaries.

Eventually we came to swampy ground; the area surrounding Latchmore is very boggy and in places dangerous. One mire, as they are called in the New Forest, stretches from Hampton Ridge down the heather-clad hillside to Latchmore where the water forms little pools, and streamlets trickle through the clay. This mire is known locally as Dirty Ditches. In the spring a drift of shimmering cotton grass cascades down the hillside and merges with an area of sphagnum moss and bog myrtle bushes. The bog myrtle, sometimes known as sweet gale, is very aromatic, and in the autumn the foliage turns to a golden russet. From the bright green moss the yellow asphodel flowers shine, and marsh orchids can be seen.

A wild place upon the heath,
Green moss with treacherous bog beneath,
Flowers of a dangerous beauty grow
In nature's garden where none dare go,
Purple orchid and asphodel
Sweet gale, ling, and heather bell,
A mist of shimmering cotton grass
Quivers in a silver mass,
The breeze in their silken tresses
With the sun gently caresses,
Shallow pools where brown trout lie,
Flowering rush and lacewing fly,

The cry of pee-wits wild and harsh
As redshanks ripple from the marsh,
Curlews call across the waste
With plaintive cry in this wild place.

A very interesting little bog plant is the sundew on account of its carnivorous habits. The leaves have bright red filaments on their upper sides, sometimes more than a hundred on each leaf. The glands on the end of each filament secrete a sticky liquid, which in the sunshine glistens like a dew-drop and attracts the insects. As soon as an insect alights on the leaf it becomes firmly stuck and, as it struggles, it comes in contact with more sticky globules until it is covered all over with the fluid. The filaments on the leaf then converge towards the captured insect and within half-an-hour it is completely covered, and then digested by the plant.

After detouring around the boggy ground and crossing watery ditches by strategically placed planks, we climbed the hill to Hasley Enclosure, passing on the way some old foxes' earths in overgrown bomb craters, relics of the last war. From the top of the hill we could see clearly across the Forest to the far horizon, and the familiar shape of Clearbury Rings in Wiltshire.

Hasley is a quiet piece of the Forest, oval in shape, and set on a hill with a sandy track right around it. As we entered the enclosure it was refreshingly cool and the air was heavy with the scent of the sweet chestnut blossom that was in profusion everywhere. There were many large chestnut trees in Hasley, and that year seemed to be exceptionally good as every tree was mantled in white. We agreed to return in the autumn with baskets to collect the chestnuts.

7 The Surrounding Forest 2

IT WAS LATE SPRING WHEN once more we walked in the deep Forest, this time venturing beyond Latchmore into Alderhill Enclosure. There were still bluebells here and there, and even the occasional violet on the banks of the stream. In places lengths of overhanging honeysuckle trailed in the water. Where the stream ran through marshy ground under self-seeded pines growing in disorder it became narrow and the banks undulating and steep. We chose this particular location in which to walk hoping to find a grass snake to photograph. Being damp and grassy it was just the kind of place they inhabit. It was necessary to bend under the branches, and leap the ditches to negotiate the water's edge.

It was in one of these ditches that we came upon a quite large grass snake. We were extremely fortunate to find one on our first trip; we fully expected to have to make several expeditions. Arthur sprang quickly and grabbed the snake before it moved and handed it to me to hold whilst he took its photograph. The snake however curled its tail up to my wrist and, feeling frightened, I let go. In a flash the creature wriggled away and shot down a hole, but not before scenting us both with an odious smelling liquid. This comes from a scent gland and is the snake's form of defence. Fortunately we were near the stream and able to wash our hands. In the few seconds that I was holding the grass snake I was able to see its colouring and markings. It was greyish olive above turning to a greenish-yellow beneath, and chequered with black. Behind its head it had two orange spots. The upper part of its body had several rows of alternate black spots.

At the far end of the marshy plantation the stream had at one time silted up and formed an ox-bow pond. This pond was oval in shape encircling a mound-like island. Growing upon the island was a dense thicket of trees, bushes, ferns and flowers, all germinated from seed blown by the wind and washed up by the water. Being out of reach of browsing animal, they had flourished. It was a paradise for birds and a safe place for nesting. There were small fir trees, gorse, willow, bracken and even one or two rhododendron bushes; foxgloves too grew there.

The pond surrounding the island had a green weed growing up through the water in places, and the edges were fringed with tall reeds and rushes. It was a very secret pond as it could not be seen until you were upon it. If you sat quietly you might catch a glimpse of a newt as it surfaced for air. Being an amphibian, this fascinating little creature spends the first part of its life as a tadpole entirely in the water but, when its transformation is complete it will take to land, though still preferring the water where it will spend most of its life. When on land newts are sometimes mistaken for lizards but a close examination will prove there is a great difference. Newts, for instance, have no scales, nor do they have nails on their toes. The newts we watched surfacing and diving in the pond were the 'smooth', or 'eft'. Their colouring was a brownish olive above, and their underparts yellowish.

We were extremely lucky that day for, whilst we were sitting silently watching the newts, we saw our second grass snake. It was swimming amongst the green weed with only its head showing, probably hunting for frogs. We watched it for a long while until eventually it swam out of sight around the far side of the pond. The grass snake is harmless, so too is the smooth snake which is also found in the Forest.

Where the surface of the pond was clear from weed, water boatmen were rowing to and fro and whirligig beetles going around in circles. When we approached nearer the pond we disturbed a pair of wild duck. It is these wild places they choose, leaving the big river in favour of the small rushy pools and boggy areas, and often they nest away from water amongst the heather and gorse. I once came upon a pair in the thick bracken of a woodland glade. It was so fascinating sitting watching the happenings in and around the water that we did not realize dusk was upon us until we began to feel chilled.

ଓଃ

As spring was now merging into summer and the weather very warm there was a need to be vigilant when walking anywhere in the Forest, for the possibility of adders. The adder has a poisonous bite which it will use if surprised or cornered. Its favourite haunt is the heathland and may often be seen coiled up in a sunny place in the shelter of a tuft of furze or heather. Its colour varies from olive-green to chocolate brown but can be distinguished by the oval-shaped spots joined together to form a zig-zag line down the middle of its back. We have on occasions come upon a sleeping adder and have quietly observed it and gone on our way without rousing it from its slumbers. To do this you must be light of foot as you approach otherwise the vibrations will alert it.

Though yet early summer, adders were already very much in evidence. This was possibly due to the hot weather having dried out the bogs and wetlands where they normally feed. They were on the move, looking for damp places such as water meadows. Arthur had recently been visiting a road reconstruction site on one of the main Forest roads where he noticed several adders. They lay in the sun on loose clumps of earth on the slopes of the embankment. This was near a piece of swampy ground where a stream had been dammed up during the construction of a new road. He said the interesting thing was they all varied considerably in colour.

One of the Forest keepers who lives at Holiday Hill near Lyndhurst has a snake pit with all the species of New Forest snakes in it. We visited it one warm sunny day as I particularly wanted to see a smooth snake – one of the Forest's rarities. To my surprise it was quite warm and dry to handle. It is a good idea to go and see all the snakes together, and become familiar with their individual markings so as to be able to identify the harmless from the poisonous.

As the summer progressed the weather was hot and dry, with just the occasional thunderstorm. Even after one of these storms the ground remained warm and soon everything was dry again. In fact it had been so dry the Forest was almost free of flies and mosquitos, making it possible to sit by a stream and picnic in the middle of July – a time when normally you would need to carry a piece of bracken to wave over your head or in front of your face to keep off the flies and midges.

ɩʒ

Picnic beside a Forest stream is exactly what we did one Saturday afternoon. We had been shopping in Salisbury Market in the morning and arrived home feeling hot and in need of the therapeutic treatment which only the peaceful Forest can provide.

The sun was hot on our backs as we pushed our bicycles up the slope of Hampton Ridge and we were glad to be on flat ground at the top to start cycling and create our own breeze. On either side of the track the heather was in full bloom; the fragrance from it filled the air and reminded one of the honey which the bees would soon be making from the nectar of this colourful flower. As the path dropped down into the enclosure another sharper scent took its place. The woodmen had been cutting down the tall Scots pines; the huge trunks lay in stacks beside the track. Their fresh cut ends were oozing a sticky resin which filled the surrounding area with this heavy perfume. Leaving the sleeping giants behind us we went deeper into the Forest where the leafy oaks provided shade, and their transpiration cooled the shafts of sunlight that penetrated to the ferns below. One of these shafts fell onto a deep pool in a Forest stream. Meandering its way through the wood this shallow stream, quite pure but stained brown from the peat, rippled between banks overhung with bracken and fern. Here and there a tree had fallen across it to provide a footbridge. In places where the stream changed course and the constant running water gouged the loose stone bed away it had formed deep pools such as the one we came upon that afternoon.

In the deepest part it was waist-high; how refreshing it was after a long cycle ride in the hot sun to slip from the grassy bank down into the depths of that silent pool. First making sure that there were not any adders swimming and hidden by overhanging vegetation.

Later whilst lying in the sun we saw a White Admiral butterfly. For some time we watched its graceful flight as it flitted from leaf to leaf on the honeysuckle. This dainty butterfly is brownish-black in colour with white bands and spots. It loves the honeysuckle and lays its eggs on the leaves. Later the caterpillar attaches a leaf to a twig with silken threads forming a chamber; inside this it will spend the winter.

There are still a few White Admiral butterflies in the forest but their numbers have fallen rapidly; at one time they were abundant in the New Forest during the months of July and August.

I think my most memorable occasion of butterflies in the Forest was whilst walking with Arthur in Hasley Enclosure. It was a warm afternoon towards the end of summer and everywhere there were Peacock butterflies. We had to slow our pace for fear of treading on them as they had found something attractive on the gravel track and were flitting up and down just above the ground and many were pitched with outstretched wings. Lulled by the warm sun they remained still, thus enabling us to see their handsome markings, distinctive from other butterflies by the 'peacock eyes' on their wings.

Numerous also in early autumn is the Red Admiral butterfly. Equally as colourful as the Peacock, it is attracted to the blossoms of the ivy, and in the cottage gardens is to be found on the Michaelmas daisies along with the hover-flies. The Comma is another butterfly on the wing in the autumn. With its ragged wings and tawny colour it loves the hedgerows at blackberry time.

The New Forest is famed for its many species of moths. One that always comes to mind is the Cinnabar, numerous in the Forest owing to the plentiful supply of ragwort. This is a plant on which the Cinnabar moth lays its eggs and will later provide food for the caterpillars. Annually the Forestry pull the ragwort just before it dies; this is when it becomes poisonous to animals, by which time the larva will have devoured most of the greenery. The caterpillars are very distinctive – their yellow and black stripes give them the appearance of little tigers. Named in 1773 because of its colour – a kind of vermilion – the Cinnabar moth is a frequent visitor to our Abbots Well garden.

When we once more set out to explore the surrounding Forest it was not to the enclosures we headed but out across the open heathland. The wild heath was in full glory with a profusion of golden gorse and purple heather, interspersed with canopies of fresh green bracken.

> *Bracken growing green and tall*
> *On the moor where curlews call,*
> *Crushed beneath the ponies' feet,*
> *A fragrance green and fresh and sweet.*

Some woodland ferns remain green all through the year. The bracken dies away in the autumn, and throws up new fronds in the spring, It is interesting to note how the fronds unfurl. At first they are coiled, similar to the top of a bishop's crosier, and covered by shaggy thin scales. Gradually the fronds unfold and lengthen out to delicate green wings.

A plover, swooping low around us, uttered a wailing cry, then, on landing, flapped about feigning a broken wing in an attempt to lure us away from its young feeding somewhere near in the undergrowth.

The gorse was in full flower and, because it blooms more or less throughout the year, there is an old saying that 'it's not kissing time when the gorse is not in bloom'. There are two species of gorse, or furze as it is called in the Forest. The common, which grows to a height of five feet or more, and the dwarf, which is a darker green, and bears flowers of a much deeper yellow.

There are several types of heather – cross-leafed heath, bell heather and ling being the most common. They are loved by bees and insects because they yield abundant supplies of sweet nectar.

The grass between the heather and gorse is closely cropped, and here and there we came upon a group of dainty harebells sheltering under tufts of furze. There were patches too of white heath bedstraw, its very heavy fragrance filling the surrounding air and competing with that of the heather. Petty whin is another shrub of the heath which grows to about twelve inches with small yellow flowers.

We were very lucky that day to see a lizard sunning itself on a bush; it even stayed long enough to be photographed but when the picture was printed the lizard was so well camouflaged it was hardly visible. A mewing sound high in the sky above us took our attention. Two buzzards were gliding and circling above, their wings outstretched with a slight upward curve. The buzzard is one of our largest hawks, and at one time became almost extinct in this country. Happily, it is now on the increase in the New Forest.

I have recollections of an incident involving a buzzard whilst walking one day in Hasley Enclosure. As I emerged from the trees into a clearing there was a tremendous 'whoosh' and 'thump', and for a split second a buzzard was on the ground just a few feet from me, its wings outstretched. Just as suddenly as it came it was gone. I had a fleeting glimpse of something in its talons as it vanished over the trees. My conclusion was that the buzzard had already started its swoop before I stepped from the trees and we both appeared simultaneously.

Climbing the hill towards Hampton Ridge we found ourselves in Dartford warbler territory. Here the gorse had grown its full height

– a lovely hideaway for the warbler or, to give it its other name, furze wren. They do indeed have all the characteristics of a wren and live and nest amongst the furze. The New Forest is one of the few habitats in this country of this elusive little bird. It was first discovered in 1773 in Dartford, Kent and that is how its name came about. The furze wren is most active in the spring when it will hop about on the tops of gorse bushes, catching moths, and other winged insects. It has an odd little song with a repetition of harsh scolding notes, and also a musical call note. We did not see any Dartfords on that day and only occasions since have we been fortunate enough to catch a glimpse of one. We have often heard them but it is quite another matter to try and locate where the sound is coming from.

Before turning for home on our heathland walk we deviated into Amberwood Enclosure to seek the cool shade of the trees. Taking a short cut from one ride to another through the bracken we noticed a baby tawny owl sitting on a low branch looking down at us through sleepy half-closed eyes. As we approached it did not attempt to move and with coaxing voice and gentle movements Arthur was able to lift it down from the tree. It made no resistance and was quite happy to sit on my hand to be photographed. Gently placing it back upon the branch we left it in peace. We were not unduly perturbed about its welfare as there was a hollow tree a few yards away where the tawnys nest every year. The tawny, or wood owl, lives in the deep woods and is the largest of the four British species. The wood owl's *too whit, too-whoo*, heard in the silence of the woods at dusk, is very impressive and affects us with a sense of mystery.

Walking under the overhanging branches of the oak trees we noticed that there were caterpillars everywhere hanging at the ends of very fine silken threads. When we shook the branch some fell to the ground but immediately climbed back up the delicate threads. Although the birds account for a great number of these caterpillars there are often enough left to completely strip the trees over a certain area. Fortunately, the oak being an enduring tree will, in a few weeks, throw another crop of leaves and by that time the caterpillars will have all changed to chrysalides or moths.

The leaves of the oak had been very early emerging in spring that year which was a promise of a good summer to come, or so the old saying would have us believe:

> *Oak before ash – summer splash,*
> *Ash before oak – summer soak.*

There are many large oaks in the Forest; perhaps the best know is the Knightwood Oak in Bolderwood Enclosure. There is also another fine example near the watersplash at Moyles Court.

In contrast to the sturdy oak is the graceful birch – 'the lady of the woods'. With its silver bole and papery bark it is numerous throughout the Forest and particularly around Abbots Well. The foliage is light and airy which enables the sunlight to filter through onto the ground beneath. If you break a branch or even a twig of the birch from March onwards the sap which is rising will pour from the wound like water from a tap. This sap is often used for making wine, but care must be taken to boil it within a few hours of being taken from the tree otherwise it will go sour. The hole in the tree where a pipe has been inserted to extract the liquid should be securely stopped or else the tree will be damaged.

In the garden there were three very tall birch trees – one weeping and two ordinary. Sadly, one spring the largest, which stood beside the garden gate, had all its leaves blackened by a late frost and this eventually killed the tree. But there was a small birch tree growing above the Wells which eventually became visible from the window and helped to fill the gap left by the old tree.

During the winter, when there are no leaves on the trees, it is possible to see clumps of twigs on some birches. These clumps, which have the appearance of crows' nests, are called witches' brooms and are brought about by a disease caused by a fungus that impedes the growth of the tree and produces a cluster of buds. There is also a bracket fungus which is exclusive to the birch called polyporus; it is white when young but turns greyish with age. Its young moist flesh becomes cork-like when mature. As Moira Savonius says in her book,

Mushrooms and Fungi, it is used by entomologists for mounting small insects in display cabinets.

ငဒ

There are many colourful fungi to be found beneath the birch trees. One example is the tawny grisette which has a shiny rich brown cap the edges of which are furrowed, and can be found from late spring till early autumn and is harmless. Another is birch boletus which has an orange-brown cap covered in tiny scales. It appears around mid-summer and continues until early autumn. This one is also edible.

One of my favourite fungi is the chanterelle. Trumpet-like with waved edges and possessing the taste and fragrance of apricots, it is a fungus reflecting the pale golden colours of autumn. It is often found growing beneath the shady canopies of russet bracken. We were delighted to find this fungus growing on the bank in the lane opposite our Abbots Well garden. The bank, being wooded by slender birch trees, had a variety of fungi growing there in the late summer and autumn. Probably the most colourful and decorative was the fly agaric, its scarlet buttons opening out to white-spotted, parasol shapes, sometimes as large as tea-plates. It is poisonous but seldom fatal.

There is a great variety of fungi growing in the New Forest. In the beech and oak woods there are puffballs with greenish-yellow skins growing amongst the fallen leaves in the autumn. There is also the violet-coloured wood blewits so loved by the gypsies. Sulphur tuft is another which is quite common. It is not only in the autumn that fungi grow, as I discovered when walking with Arthur in the deep Forest one evening towards the end of July. The day had been oppressively hot, but the evening brought a slight breeze and beneath the trees it was quite cool. The bracken had grown very tall, in some places shoulder-high. However, pushing our way through we came to the banks of a partly dried up brook along the edge of which was a wire fence separating the enclosures. Eventually locating the gate and entering the enclosure we found ourselves in the dank musty part of the Forest where the sun seldom manages to penetrate the thick mantle of leaves overhead. Beneath our feet were as many leaves again, fallen and collected over the years to form a crisp carpet.

It was here under the trees, where the air was damp and all was silent, that we discovered one of nature's hidden gardens. Walking through the drab dead leaves we came upon many differently coloured fungi standing out brightly against their sombre background. There was the ginger-brown devil's boletus, the scarlet cap of the sickener, false chanterelle, a bright yellow toadstool and various other species in purple and olive-green – all very beautiful but some poisonous.

On another occasion whilst looking for fungi in an enclosure close by Sloden we came upon some fragments of pottery lying on top of the ground. These were pieces of Roman pottery. In certain places there is so much that the moles throw it up when they dig and it can be found on top of their mounds. We have visited many times since the various sites where there are fragments to be found by scuffing the light loamy soil with your feet. Arthur's prize find was a flat piece of brownish pottery perforated all over with small holes – a Roman sieve perhaps? My favourite was the neck of a pot or oil flask. This I found was large enough to hold a candle, so I stuck it to the base of a pot which I also found and made a candlestick. I had many interesting finds including two more necks of oil flasks but they were very small.

A few years after we moved to Abbots Well there was an important find when the Forestry Commission was constructing a road through one of the enclosures close to Old Sloden. They unearthed a Roman kiln intact and complete with pots in position for firing. The pots were removed and are now in Salisbury Museum, the kiln was buried again and the road laid over the top of it.

There was much to discover in the surrounding Forest but I think for me the mysterious whirring of the nightjars at dusk on warm spring evenings was something very special. That fascinating sound being difficult to pinpoint as at one moment it appears so close, then so far away. Abbots Well, situated as it is on a wooded corner which merges into the surrounding Forest with wild heathland on three sides of it, we are naturally close to the purring trill of nightjars. There is no need to go outside as they can be heard simply by opening the window; but to walk amongst them on the heathland is a unique experience.

It is best to choose a clear warm evening at sunset as we did one evening in early June. At first we could only hear the whirring, but as our eyes became accustomed to the fading light, we could see the occasional silhouette of this secretive bird briefly perched on a bare stump of burnt gorse wood. After a few seconds the shadowy form silently continued its moth-like flight, wheeling this way and that on an eccentric course. Then out of the darkness came another nightjar to join it, and with graceful sweeps both birds continued their erratic flight, all the while uttering a soft *co-ic*, and then a sharp repeated alarm *quik, quik*. This was obviously a courtship flight as they seemed oblivious of us and flew very close. One surprised us when it cracked its wings, sounding like a gun-shot. They do this by raising their wings vertically and bringing them down sharply to produce a noise which can be frightening if you are not expecting it. All too soon the sun sank beneath the horizon and darkness enveloped the surrounding Forest, and as we made our way home the mysterious whirrings faded into the night.

8 Forest Folk

A FEW DAYS AFTER MOVING to Abbots Well we met our forester neighbour Len Witt. He had lived in the village for nearly seventy-eight years, and could tell many a good tale. These stories we were to hear as time went by for Len loved to talk and half-an-hour would soon pass in his interesting company. He possessed a fantastic memory for dates, and the weather over the years. He could tell you that in "1911 there were three drizzly days in June, a thunderstorm in August, then it was dry until November." Or how sixty-eight years ago, on his tenth birthday, "Wednesday to be exact," he was "up in Forest" when there was a terrible thunderstorm and "the brook in Latchmore Bottom was filled up and the water ran over the top of the bridge, but after that it was a beautiful summer."

Len had a large red cow called Dolly which he would lead up and down the lane on the end of a piece of rope. She was a sad looking cow – her horns were at different angles and her hooves had grown long through spending so much time on boggy ground. In the mornings Len would take Dolly to the well to drink, after which he would either put her into the water meadow below the garden or turn her on the Forest. In summer, if the cow was on the Forest she would be so tormented by flies that in the afternoon she would go home. Walking slowly back up the lane she always paused at the bank opposite our gate to see if there were any cabbage leaves put out for her.

The old forester had been looking after cows since he was ten. He had owned Dolly for sixteen years and her mother before her. Despite her age Dolly was a very fit cow and had produced a calf every year until she was fifteen. When about to calf she would hide herself away in the thickest part of the furze, and poor Len would spend hours looking for her. He came to the gate one evening so worried because she was due to calf and he could not find her. Arthur looked through his binoculars and could see what he thought to be Dolly's head protruding above the gorse on Chilly Hill. Together they went to look and eventually found her in a dense clump of furze and bracken; she had calved but had her offspring hidden somewhere in the thicket so another search was started. It was an hour before the calf was found and it took them as long again to get it clear of the undergrowth by which time Arthur was covered in scratches – tired and dusty.

Dolly was not a good mother as she would go home leaving her calf asleep somewhere on the Forest. I remember one afternoon, when Len had gone to market, seeing Mrs. Witt, in Wellington boots and wearing an apron, with a stick driving the cow back down the lane to her calf, but as soon as she turned for home Dolly followed her back up the lane again. Three times this happened and eventually Mrs. Witt had to fetch the calf herself and drive it home.

All Dolly's bedding was dried bracken. In the autumn Len would spend several days with a hand hook cutting the golden bracken from the side of Windmill Hill. He gathered it into small bundles which he carried home one at a time in a rope sling on his back. The bracken was then dried and stacked, thus providing a good supply of bedding throughout the winter.

Apart from looking after his cow Len grew strawberries and at one time he travelled by horse and cart to Southampton and Bournemouth to sell them. I often heard him tell of how many years ago he travelled regularly along Hampton Ridge by moonlight in his horse and cart. Sometimes it was as late as one o'clock in the morning after a day selling his strawberries in Southampton. He would fall asleep in the bottom of the cart and the horse would find its own way home. Usually there was a bag of sovereigns on board but never once was he robbed.

Strawberries have always been grown in the Forest villages. The meadow below our garden was once a strawberry field. There is an old saying that the air that blows over the forest smells of strawberries and honey.

oß

On moving to Abbots Well I was delighted to discover that living in the nearby village of Godshill was artist, potter and sculptor Sid Finch. Sid was a colleague of my father – the well known Salisbury artist Frederick Wilton. Both artists enjoyed creating constructional pictures which they regularly exhibited. Together with another Salisbury artist they formed a small painting group with the express purpose of holding outdoor exhibitions; it was called The Progressive Group of Artists. With just a limited number of members it proved very successful. Outdoor exhibitions were held at various locations in Salisbury, amongst them the George Mall, Guildhall Square and the Cathedral Cloisters. It was the exhibition held in the beautiful setting of the Cloisters that I remember best. As well as exhibiting his paintings, Sid Finch had on show several pieces of pottery and sculpture. He also had his potter's wheel and was demonstrating the art of throwing a pot.

I can recall the evening we visited Sid Finch in his wooden house situated in a pine wood. It was dusk as we made our way down the path between the trees. When we arrived Sid hurried us through to the window at the side of the house to see the sunset through the pines. From there the view overlooked the Avon valley and, far below us through the tops of the trees, we caught a glimpse of silver which was the river lazily gliding along. As the sun sank below the horizon we turned our backs on this scene to return to the cosiness of the living-room. A large sofa stretched before a stove ablaze with logs, filling the room with the smell of woodsmoke. On the table was a pottery bowl filled with golden russet apples blushed with red, a reminder that it was autumn.

Around the walls hung some of Sid's pictures – heavy ceramic compositions. He also did fine pottery using clay from the Forest; we saw some examples of his work during the evening. I already owned a piece of his pottery in the form of a large brown cider jar with a huge wooden bung. It was kept on top of a milking stool and was in fact one of my prize possessions.

Apart from Sid's painting and pottery he was also a qualified carpenter and had recently done a remarkable restoration task on an old gypsy caravan. The van was a Reading over a hundred and thirty years old, a fine example in magnificent colours. The Reading vans were very tall and made completely from wood; they were beautifully carved and painted. It was not easy to come by one as it was a tradition to burn the van after the death of the occupier.

Coming home that night from our visit to Sid Finch we met Len walking down the road with a torch. He said he had put Dolly on the Forest as usual that morning but she had not come home and he was quite sure she was lying injured somewhere or fallen into a bog.

The following morning Dolly was still missing. For four days we searched everywhere. Mrs. Witt said Len could not sleep at night for worrying about her, imagining she had been stolen by cattle thieves. On the morning of the fifth day I saw the cow walking over Windmill Hill with a rope hanging from her horns and, running up the hill to tell Len, I found him hot and exhausted. He said that morning he had found Dolly a long way off in the next valley with another herd of cows and he had tried to lead her home and push his bicycle at the same time but she proved too strong for him and broke loose. Nevertheless that same afternoon the cow came home of her own accord with the rope still hanging from her horns.

❀

Another acquaintance of my Wiltshire days I discovered living nearby in the village. When Ron Coombes and his father drove their horse and cart from Fordingbridge up to Salisbury every Saturday to sell fresh vegetables and fruit, my mother was one of their customers. I remember it was always lunch-time when they reached our house and time for the horse to have its nosebag. Ron was a shy young man with never much to say. His father, on the other hand, was a stem man immaculately dressed with polished gaiters and a waxed moustache. The cart was well turned out with a long-handled whip resting in a bracket on the side of the cart, slightly protruding so that the traffic would have to keep their distance. The produce was all neatly stacked. I often wondered how it survived the journey but in those days things were done in a more leisurely way. I think the cart suffered more from an angry neighbour who tried to tip it over spilling the fruit, vegetables and eggs all over the road after a disagreement with Mr. Coombes.

Mr. Coombes had now died and Ron was living alone in the family cottage just down the hill from Abbots Well. When I visited him there I was fascinated to see many relics of the Forest from former days. Nothing had been altered, even the polished leather gaiters that Ron's father always wore when driving the horse and cart were still hanging on a hook in a shed. There was also a cart that the horse pulled for moving timber when Ron worked 'up in Forest.'

The cottage itself was a typical New Forest dwelling of earlier days. It was a long, low, single-storeyed, thatched building incorporating a dairy at one end. Beside the dairy was a shed which provided cover for an old, deep, bricked well which at one time was their source of fresh water. Towards the side of the garden was an intriguing looking outhouse which had a bricked chimney. Inside there was a big copper with a cast iron bowl where, according to Ron, they cooked up potatoes for the pigs. Most foresters kept a few pigs to supply them with meat during the winter. Inside yet another outhouse was the old trough used for salting the pig after slaughter. There were also rows of shelves where the apples from the large orchard were stored. Outside, against the side of the shed, was a lean-to and stacked beneath it were bundles and bundles of furze for firewood. These had the appearance of having been there for many years.

On entering the cottage through the low doorway you were plunged into darkness until their eyes became accustomed. The windows were small and the ceiling low, although the room itself was quite sizeable with a large inglenook fireplace where once upon a time a long chain supported a cooking pot over the fire.

೦೩

Formerly the New Forest gypsies were allowed to roam and camp freely. In recent years they have been turned off the Forest and have either gone elsewhere or moved into permanent accommodation. One of the largest Romany families that live in and around the Forest are the Coopers. When we first moved to Abbots Well Eiza Cooper called occasionally to ask for old clothes. She was a remarkable lady who in her eighties was still working at a market garden hoeing the weeds from between the rows of vegetables.

At the same time living in a caravan tucked away amongst the gorse on Hyde Common was Annie Cooper, and nearby her sister Caroline. Annie, who walked to Fordingbridge every day, was always very colourfully dressed in a long floral skirt and bright apron. Sometimes she would be pushing a pram brimming over with flowers or, at Christmas time, holly. I have vivid memories of seeing these folk gathering moss from around Abbots Well and the side of Chilly Hill to use in the foundations of the holly wreaths they made at Christmas.

As with all Romanies Annie loved her many ponies, her favourite being an old grey mare called 'Feather'. She was often out on the common at five o'clock in the morning if the mare had failed to come home the night before. Sadly, now both Annie and her sister Caroline have died but there are sons, daughters and grandchildren to carry on the Cooper family and Romany way of life.

೦೩

One grey November afternoon I was walking by the wells with my mother and her dog when we met Len. He was having difficulty leading a high spirited heifer up the hill on the end of a rope. I asked him where Dolly was as I had not seen her for a while. It was a great shock when he replied: "she's a gonner, she went last Wednesday." Although he had been talking about getting rid of her for a year or more, we did not think he really would. He said she was seventeen years old and if he was taken ill there would be no one to look after her. We realized we would not see again her familiar figure grazing on Windmill Hill, sitting in the sun on the corner by the wells, or walking slowly up the hill on her way home at the end of the day.

As Len was the strawberry grower in the village so Charlie Chalke was the cider maker in the neighbouring village of Blissford. Charlie was a market gardener and recalls the time when he used to drive his horse and cart to Ringwood with a load of vegetables sometimes as early as six in the morning. Charlie had been making cider for as long as he could remember but it was not until 1938 that he bought the cider mill on wheels and began making cider in a big way. Sometimes he made as much as two hundred gallons in one year.

Cider-making was at one time carried out all over the Forest as most cottages had an orchard on their land. Not every cottager had his own press and an old man called Hiscocks would bring one around the villages on a horse-drawn waggon.

❧

These are only a few of the Forest folk that I have met over the years. Born in the Forest, they have lived there most of their lives except for those who had an enforced break to serve during the war. Some who were too young or for other reasons stayed home and became members of the New Forest Mounted Division of the Home Guard. There were only two other mounted units in the country. Although uniforms were supplied, most members of the platoon rode their own horses for which they received a corn allowance. There are still two surviving members living in the village today.

I regret not having met a lady who, though not Forest-born, later became very much a part of it. Her name was Barbara de Seyssel and she lived alone in a remote cottage situated in a clearing inside a wooded enclosure at Holmhill. She first came to the New Forest in the 1960s to work with the Pony Patrol. This was a group of horse riders who kept watch to ensure that the ponies did not stray too close to the Lyndhurst and Ringwood roads. These were the days before cattle grids were installed and fences built. On occasions some ponies have slipped past the Patrol's watchful eyes – I have seen them in the centre of Lyndhurst.

I did not know of Barbara de Seyssel until one day whilst riding with a friend she told of how periodically she made a trek across the Forest to visit this extraordinary woman. She explained how the inside of her cottage was primitive, with only one room habitable as very often there would be the odd bale of hay for the ponies stored in the others. She recalled how on one occasion, after returning from a horseback shopping expedition to the village, she sat on an upturned box and drank tea from a baked bean tin.

Barbara de Seyssel was a well educated lady; her father was a Major General in the Army and her mother a beautiful American artist. She cared little for her own comfort but all her energy went into looking after her animals, ponies, hens, cat and beloved collie Bonny. Before being able to accompany my friend on one of her periodical visits, Barbara de Seyssel died suddenly. I was saddened at having missed meeting her.

Sadly now there are not many of these characters left and, as one by one they fade away, their cottages are sold for conversion and modernization. A lot of them are used for weekend and holiday homes which means most of the year they are standing empty. One cottage situated on the side of a hill had at one time pigstys attached. During modernization these were removed and, although the conversion was done tastefully, the entire character and authenticity was lost.

When Ron Coombes left his cottage for a smaller home it was completely demolished, together with all the outhouses, and a modern bungalow was built on the land; yet another old Forest dwelling gone for good.

9 The Forest Animals

With tossing mane and trailing tail
Wild ponies tread the fragrant gale,
With gentle hoof on sphagnum moss
The marshy ground they safely cross;
'Neath leafy branches green and cool
Wild ponies drink from forest pool,
They wander free o'er heather and bog
In summer sun and winter fog.

Probably the picture which comes to mind at the mention of the New Forest is that of the ponies. They appear on postcards and calendars and are the subject of every tourist's snapshot. As they are running free they give the impression of being wild but each one has an owner and carries a brand-mark to prove it. These brand marks are not always visible in the winter when their coats are long; it is necessary for the hair to be snipped to find the mark.

The original Forest pony was sturdy and able to exist in the deep

Forest all year round, even during hard weather. It grows a thick coat in winter, and long hair around the face especially on its upper lip. This moustache forms a protection when the pony is eating gorse. To feed from this prickly bush they curl back their lips onto their molars. The holly is also part of their diet but they prefer the tender young shoots at the ends of the branches. Holly trees have a way of protecting themselves by producing very prickly leaves on the lower branches, leaving the smoother ones which are out of the ponies' reach at the top.

Unfortunately in Victorian times an Arabian stallion was turned onto the Forest thus producing a much softer breed of pony. Most of them are now unable to fend for themselves during the hard weather in winter and have to be fed hay or straw, though not all the ponies need their diet supplemented as there are still some of the hardier ones left. A group of these range from Abbots Well and I know of three – two chestnuts and one grey which grow long moustaches in winter.

The diet of these ponies varies according to the season. When grass is limited in the Forest they browse the gorse and holly. It was at one time believed that ponies did not eat bracken but in the deep Forest you will find groups of ponies cropping the green fronds in preference to the grass growing beneath. I have seen a pony having a bracken sandwich. It first cropped several fronds of bracken then a few mouthfuls of the water herbs which were growing in the stream beneath the hedge, then more bracken. It is not unusual to see a pony standing up to its belly in mud and water eating wild watercress and other water herbs. There was a mare doing this very thing in the wetlands at North Gorley one morning when Arthur was passing in the car. He noticed that her foal had followed her in and was up to its neck in mud and unable to move. Arthur stopped the car, got out, put on his boots and grabbed a tow rope. Going into the bog he managed to get the rope around the foal's neck but the mare, thinking he was attacking her little one, lashed out at him. He tried to move but his boots were stuck fast. If it had not been for the quick action of a man from the farm close by, who came to his rescue and kept the mare at bay with a pitchfork, I dare not think what might of happened. Arthur was eventually able to rescue the foal and also his wellies.

It is not often a Forest pony will venture near any of the treacherous bogs which are numerous in the Forest. They seem to have and inbuilt instinct and will detour around them and, as they range only a few miles from their home area, they become familiar with the terrain.

Spring is perhaps one of the best times of the year for the ponies as they can enjoy the sunshine without the tormenting flies which come with summer. In spring too the new foals arrive. It is always interesting to watch the mares leave the village in the evenings and make their way up Hampton Ridge to the open Forest where they spend the night, and to see them return again in the morning with perhaps a new foal born overnight running with them.

Evening is the time when all young animals become lively and like to play. Lambs will leave the ewes and gather together at the edge of the field where they race back and forth, one or two occasionally leaping into the air from sheer exuberance. The same applies to ponies - whilst the mares are having their last graze before night the foals will gallop around in circles, first in one direction then in the opposite. These ritual gallops are punctuated by a kick and a buck and sometimes a stumble when they turn too fast for their long wobbly legs.

During the summer the stallions are turned onto the Forest. These animals must now be of the Forest breed, registered and passed by a vet. Each stallion has his own territory and group of mares. It is a lovely sight to see him rounding up the mares which have strayed too far. He will gallop through the heather with his head down, neck arched, ears back. The mares, sometimes reluctant to return to the group go galloping away with mane and tail streaming in the wind, but eventually they are overtaken and turned around.

Should a stallion wander onto another's territory he will immediately be seen off. Sometimes the stranger will challenge him whereupon they will rear up on their hind legs and paw out at each other uttering sharp whinnies as they do so. Although they give the impression of being fiery creatures to be kept well clear of, there was one stallion which ran with the mares from Abbots Well all year round. He was docile and friendly and regularly came to our gate to have his nose rubbed.

During our early days at Abbots Well there was a group of mares – all one family – which belonged to Mr. Marlow, a forester from the village. There was Polly, who was very old, her daughter Frosty and her foal Kitty, who was special to us as she was born the same month as our wedding. She never did grow to be a big pony but remained slender and dainty and when she herself had a foal that too was small. Kitty was very friendly and on occasions we would let her with her foal into the orchard to graze the grass when it grew long. She was timid and could easily be driven out when we considered she had had enough. Later there was another pony born into the same group that was deep chestnut with a honey-colour tail and mane. Not only was her colouring striking but her mane was long and thick, and her tail reached the ground. Appropriately her name was 'Treacle'.

This group of ponies seldom passed the gate without stopping to hang their heads over it for a few minutes to see if there were any titbits to be had, an apple or crust of bread. Old Polly was an inveterate scrounger. The milkman once shared his sandwiches with her and after that when she saw his milk-van she would follow him along the road as he stopped at each house.

Overhanging from the garden onto the Forest is an old willow tree, one branch of which is only a few feet from the ground. It is just the right height for the ponies to stand beneath and rub their backs. We call it the scratching tree, and when they do so we can see from the window the top of the tree shaking. It is particularly popular with them in spring when they are losing their long winter coats. At that time of year there is always a carpet of hair on the ground beneath the tree.

One winter the ponies nearly lost their precious scratching tree when two men came with a bow-saw. We had visitors and Arthur, having gone into the kitchen to make coffee, saw the tree shaking. However, it was not ponies under it but two men, one of whom was sawing at the branch. Arthur dashed into the garden and through the Forest gate whereupon the two men ran to a car and drove off. The reason we think was they were collecting wood for bonfire-night as it was November the fourth. The ponies scratching tree was saved but Arthur slipped on the mud when he ran through the gate and fell with his leg under him. He spent the rest of the day in the hospital casualty ward and was in great pain with his knee for many weeks.

There is a contagious disease called strangles which attacks the younger ponies. The older ones too are susceptible if they escape it in their youth. It is very distressing to see a young pony which is suffering from strangles. We came across a yearling on the Forest once that was in the throes of this frightening illness. Its nose was streaming with catarrh, there were abscess swellings by the jaw bone, and it appeared to be in great distress. We rang the agister when we got home and he assured us that the illness was rarely dangerous and that the pony was best left where it was for as soon as the abscess bursts and drains there is instant relief. Apparently with this disease it is best in the long term not to treat it with drugs but just let it take its course.

⍥

The agisters are appointed by the Verderers to look after the welfare of the ponies and cattle. There are four and each one has his particular area of the Forest to cover. If a lame or injured animal is reported to the agister he will go to its aid and take it off the Forest. With every animal being branded with the commoners' own markings it is not difficult to trace the owner who will then be responsible for treating it. The agisters have an official livery for special occasions; this includes a dark green coat which I believe is a very expensive item of clothing. They looked very impressive on horseback wearing their livery the day that the Queen and Prince Philip visited the New Forest. It was the occasion of the celebration to mark the 900th anniversary of the founding of the New Forest.

All the agisters are naturally excellent riders to be able to carry out their duties. In the autumn when the 'Drift', or round-up, takes place they ride with the commoners to round up the ponies. Needless to say, the green coats are not worn for this; they will most likely be in shirt sleeves and jeans, or cords. It is an impressive sight to see both agister and commoner handling their horses in the Round Up. Great skill is needed for the speed they have to ride over rough ground, treacherous with hidden rabbit holes and ant hills, whilst at the same time having to manoeuvre between gorse bushes to head off the ponies. At Abbots Well when the Drift is in progress the ponies come galloping off the Forest and up the lane followed by the horsemen shouting and cracking their whips, at which time it is prudent to keep well clear.

The ponies are driven into a pound next to the Foresters Arms where they are separated into small groups. Some are to go to the Beaulieu Roads sales whilst others are to be wormed, checked out by the vet, and have their tales clipped. The ponies have chunks of hair cut from their tails to indicate that the owners have paid their dues for keeping them on the Forest. The cutting is carried out by the agister (agister is a word of Norman derivation meaning to receive payment) who has to go into the compound and stand behind these wild and sometimes kicking ponies to do this. Each agister has his own pattern for cutting the tail so that it can be seen at a glance that not only has the commoner paid his dues but also which area the pony ranges in.

All ponies and cattle must be branded with their owner's mark before they can graze upon the Forest. Ponies are traditionally branded on the left side, usually on the shoulder but sometimes on the back or hip. When a pony changes owners a new brand must be made as it is illegal to brand on top of an old one. Every owner has his own brand-mark; some are initials whilst others are symbols. There is a bar at the Green Dragon Inn at Brook where all the brand marks are displayed on sheets of leather hanging around the walls.

The time of year the Forest ponies are seen at their best is probably in the late summer and early autumn as they stand in the deep heather or russet bracken with the evening sun highlighting their rich coats. I have the pleasure of seeing them gather around the wells to drink on their way to and from to the open Forest all the year round.

ભ

The cattle too come under the protection of the agisters. They are also branded but have ear-tags to indicate that the dues for their grazing rights have been paid. They now remain on the Forest all the year round, but at one time they were brought in during the winter from 22nd November to 4th May following; this custom was known as Winter Hayning, and the reason was to preserve the keep for the deer.

In former days the peasant would keep a few cattle that would graze on the forest for part of the year and would eventually provide him with a supply of beef. This beef he would salt down and store for use during the winter months.

At one time the cows wore bells around their necks as did the sheep on the Wiltshire Downs. When we first came to the forest we used to see a cow wearing a bell grazing near Picket Post, a very rare sight now. I loved to see her wandering through the heather with her bell tinkling and when walking in the area you could always tell where she was. The bells must have been a great help to the forester of former days when rounding up his cattle.

Our neighbour Jim Loader has a fine herd of cows which he runs on the Forest during winter and spring. Every morning he drives them down the lane and onto the open Forest where they spend the day grazing the heather shoots and sitting in the sun until late afternoon when they slowly walk down Hampton Ridge and back up the lane. Both on the way out to the Forest and on their return home they are always led by the cow which we call lead-cow. If she stops for any reason – to graze or scratch on the scratching tree the others will wait until she leads the way once more.

The ivy has a great attraction for the cows – they will always stop if any has been put outside after gardening. There is none left growing below the browsing line on the hedges around the garden. As Len Witt used to say: "'tis doctor and the cows seem to know this." The one thing ivy cannot cure for them though is forest eye. This is a condition of the eyes caused by flies, making them weep and bringing infection which causes blindness. It can be cured but it is a long process.

A number of years ago we were driving along the road across the big open lawn near the ornamental drive at Brockenhurst when a young heifer staggered into the road in front of the car. It gave the impression of being drunk but, on investigation, we found it to be totally blind -both eyes were bulged and opaque, and were weeping badly. For a moment we were puzzled as to what to do; it was obvious that the animal could not be left. Arthur, having worked on a farm as a boy and knowing how to handle animals, caught hold of its horns and with a quick jerk threw it sideways onto the ground and then sat on its neck to keep it down whilst I drove to a telephone. Within fifteen minutes the agister arrived with a horse-box, and took the poor creature away for treatment.

During the outbreak of foot and mouth disease it was not possible to bring all the cattle off the Forest so an enormous compound was made on Hampton Ridge for this area. Hundreds of cattle were fenced in and fodder was taken to them daily by tractor. Fortunately they escaped the disease and were once again given their freedom to roam the Forest.

❧

The New Forest is famed for its wild deer and unlike the ponies and cattle the deer are not owned by anyone. For this reason they do not come under the protection of the agisters, but are the responsibility of the Forest keepers. During the hard winter months, when food is scarce, the keepers will cut down holly branches for the deer to browse, and potatoes are fed to the herds in the sanctuary.

In former days it was the red deer that roamed the Forest. In 1079 when William the Conqueror established the New Forest as his own exclusive hunting ground, it was the red deer, together with the wild boar, that the King and his nobles pursued, and this sport continued until the Deer Removal Act 1871. The intention was to remove all the deer from the Forest but fortunately this was never carried out as it proved an impossible task although the herds were greatly diminished.

There are now very few red deer left in the Forest, only two small herds, and these are not hunted. They have become very shy and live quietly, hidden in a wild part of the Forest surrounded by mires which makes it fairly inaccessible. On one occasion we did stalk the red deer with a camera but it was a long while before we could find them and as long again to creep up close enough to take photographs.

There was an exciting few minutes once whilst driving across the Forest near Lymington when five or six red deer ran over the road in front of the car. We had experienced the same thing a few years before that near Balmer Lawn, but it is a very rare occurrence.

During the days of William the Conqueror there was a lot of poaching carried out, often by cruel means, such as an apple on a hook hanging from a tree. A story told by an old forester neighbour of ours was that he could remember a man once living in Abbots Well Cottage who, having shot a deer, dragged it indoors and hid it in bed with his wife. When the police arrived they were unable to find anything as they did not think of searching the bed. He went on to tell of another man who killed a deer and brought it indoors and put it in front of the fire. His wife fetched pillows and blankets to cover it over and put her two small children on top, telling them to 'bide quiet till the police had gone'.

Poaching, alas, is still carried out in the Forest. 'Lamping', the method now used, involves the use of four-wheel drive vehicles with searchlights and lurcher dogs. In the old days, to prevent dogs from harming the deer, there was the 'lawing' of dogs which meant that three toes of their fore feet were mutilated to prevent them from running fast enough to catch a deer. The lawing only applied if the dog was too big to pass through the measure. This measure was a Tudor relic known as the 'Stirrup of Rufus' and can be seen hanging in the New Forest Museum at Lyndhurst.

It is the fallow which are now hunted in the Forest and they are the most numerous. Buck hunting is a very outdated and cruel pastime, for a pastime is all that it is. It has nothing to do with control for the keepers cull the deer and this is done by a clean shot and the animal dies instantly. During hunting the buck is chased for some hours until it is exhausted and can go no further whereupon it comes to a standstill and is surrounded by baying hounds. A huntsman then approaches the buck and shoots it in the head.

Arthur was driving along the Forest road above Linwood one day when he saw what he thought was a puff of smoke rolling across the heather, then realized it was an animal travelling in its own cloud of steam. It was a buck in such a state of exhaustion that its tongue was hanging out and, as it crossed the track, it tried to lap water from a puddle but could not stop as the hounds were only a hundred yards behind it. How can anyone justify this torment to one of God's creatures? Not only does the hunted buck suffer, but the does too are harassed. We once saw from our window hounds chasing does which were running with the hunted buck. When the huntsmen called the hounds off the pack split up and there were hounds chasing both buck and does all over the place. It must be taken into consideration also that the does were carrying fawns at that time of the year.

There is no excuse for hunting as a means to provide venison and the meat from a hunted deer is useless anyhow. There are some New Forest butchers who have game licenses to sell venison of humanely killed deer.

The coat of the fallow deer is brown in winter and chestnut with white spots in summer. These colours vary, however, for there are a few light honey colour does, and at one time in the Abbots Well area there was a white buck. Over the years, whilst walking in the Forest, we have seen hundreds of deer but there was one animal above all others which has stayed in my memory. This was a magnificent black buck which I encountered just before dusk one evening, standing on the edge of a ride in Amberwood Enclosure. The light being poor it was not quite sure if I was human or just a post as I froze and tried to merge into the background. It lifted one leg as if to move but curiosity kept it staring in my direction. Suddenly it was off and with great leaps went bounding away through the long bracken. This had been one of those very special moments.

Quite often the deer will come off the Forest after dark and go onto agricultural land especially when food is scarce. One bright moonlight night we heard what we thought was a dog bark in the meadow behind the house. Looking from the landing window we saw illuminated by the moon a buck with a herd of does feeding in the field just below the window. The noise we had heard was the gutteral alarm call of the deer, a sound we often heard in the deep Forest.

There was one particular herd with several buck amongst them that regularly left the Forest in daylight and made their way to a field near us where they grazed and sat in the sun only a hundred yards from the road. One morning as we were driving past we had to pull the car up suddenly when they leapt over the wire fence and across the road in front of us, having been disturbed by something. One buck did not jump high enough and got caught in the wire but soon freed itself and went bounding after the others, seemingly unhurt.

Roe deer are numerous in the Forest but are not as gregarious as the fallow. A roe buck will mark its territory by bark stripping, this is done by tearing the bark of young trees with its teeth around the perimeter of its area. After it has established its own small piece of the forest it will stay there for most of the time apart from the winter when the roe tend to form small groups. If another buck should stray onto another's territory it will be seen off in no uncertain manner. I was walking with Arthur in Hasley Enclosure one afternoon in late summer when I left the track and climbed the bank to pick some heather. Suddenly there was a crashing of bushes and a thumping of hooves as two roe buck came racing by missing me by inches. That was clearly a case of one being seen off the other's territory.

Although smaller than the fallow, the roe is both a powerful leaper and a fast runner, in fact it is Britain's fastest land mammal over a maintained distance and can cover fifteen to twenty miles at a speed of twenty-five miles per hour. It shows no effort when jumping. I was walking along a Forest track which had a wood on one side and bramble bushes with a steep incline on the other when out from the trees came a roe, and with grace and ease leapt across the track, over the bushes, landed down the incline and carried on its way.

Due to the roe's ability to jump fences they sometimes find their way into gardens where they do considerable damage. They have a passion for roses which was demonstrated when they raided our neighbour's garden and ate their prize blooms. We could not understand why our little wood looked so bare until we realized that all the ivy leaves had been eaten by the deer. Overhead there were bare stems hanging, and underfoot just the woody stalks instead of a green carpet. Like other animals, deer seem to know the medicinal value of ivy. We erected a high fence between our own and neighbour's garden; the overhead branches reaching down to the top of it made it impossible for anything to jump over.

The roe seemed to prefer things of beauty for their food, such as roses and the lovely pink campion flowers. I am thinking in particular of a bluebell wood outside the Forest that had its trees cut down – it was on a hillside and the trees had been hazel and ash. Just a few ash trees were left standing but the following spring the bluebells bloomed followed by drifts of pink campion. Each evening several roe deer would emerge from the fir copse at the top of the rise and work their way down through the flowers occasionally being hidden behind the hazel stools that were throwing shoots again. It was a very pretty picture to see the deer in their rich chestnut summer pelage standing amongst the flowers, devouring the pink blooms of the campion.

There are two further species of deer in the New Forest, namely sika and muntjac, both of which have been established only since the 1900s after escaping from private collections. The sika, which originate from Eastern Asia, can be found in the south of the Forest in Frame and surrounding enclosures. On the two occasions that we walked in Frame the sky was overcast which added to the dreariness of the surrounding woodland. Although we saw a number of deer, the photographs we shot were poor due to the bad light.

The muntjac, which are also from Eastern Asia, are our smallest deer, standing only about eighteen inches at the shoulder, and as they walk with their heads down the hindquarters tend to be higher. They are very elusive little deer and have been sighted in the Forest by only a few people. Mark Ash is one of their confirmed haunts and it was here that Arthur and I walked one damp afternoon. Autumn had only just merged into winter and the larches were still a golden yellow although their needles were falling fast. Underfoot the discarded needles made a silent spongy carpet to walk upon. Soon we were out of the larch wood and into a more sombre woodland where ancient trees formed a canopy overhead. Tall beeches, oaks and ash grew side by side with towering Scots pine. The lower cover comprised of birches, holly, alder, and here and there a hazel tree. A valley ran down the centre of the wood with a brook meandering and trickling its way along, with miniature waterfalls cascading down into small pools. The surrounding ground was bog with carpets of sphagnum moss, and everywhere decayed wood lay around from fallen trees of long ago, a paradise for wood ants. Some dead trunks were still standing and these had been well drilled by woodpeckers whilst tree creepers were busy on some smaller dead holly stumps.

Leaving the bog and climbing up the bracken-covered banks we reached drier ground where we could follow the track above the valley. The ground cover on this path, apart from patches of coarse grass, was bilberry and white fork moss cushions. Eventually we came to a small plantation with very rough tufty ground which showed all the signs of the presence of muntjac. The bark of the smaller trees were stripped near the base and all around there were little heaps of droppings but the deer themselves were nowhere to be seen. However, we were suddenly startled by a sharp bark close by in the long bracken. We thought at last we were going to catch a glimpse of this very secretive little deer but we were disappointed when silence once again prevailed without even a movement of the bracken to indicate its whereabouts.

When walking in the Forest in the spring we always look to see if we can find a cast antler but so well disguised are they when they fall upon the Forest floor that we have not so far been lucky. Also the deer themselves sometimes nibble them to extract nutrients such as calcuim and phosphorus. As soon as the old antlers are cast the new ones begin to grow and these are covered in velvet. By the end of the summer the velvet begins to dry and strip off. The deer will eventually clean the antlers completely by rubbing them against low branches. When the velvet is in the process of coming off it can give an untidy look to the deer. One evening we were sitting quietly over a badger sett in Hasley when a grazing fallow buck came very close. Suddenly it was aware of us and lifted its head quickly and, as it stared in our direction, we thought it had a piece of rope entwined and hanging from its antlers until we realized it was strips of velvet. It is the red, fallow and sika deer which cast their antlers in the spring, the roe loose theirs at the end of the year and grow their new ones over the winter.

ം

For me the animal which always comes to mind in connection with the New Forest is the wild boar. I think probably that is why I love to see the pigs on the Forest during pannage. At that time my thoughts wander to the possibility of wild boar once more roaming the New Forest. William the Conqueror and his nobles hunted them on horseback. They used a long spear, an example of which can be seen at the New Forest Museum in Lyndhurst.

The highlight of many a pompous feast was the entrance of the boar's head resting on a silver platter – with a flower tucked behind one ear and menacing tusks it looked both frivolous and ferocious.

ം

10 Rose Cottage

Disaster struck the cottage during the heavy snow of one bad winter. The thatch collapsed under the weight which put the entire building in peril. Without the protection of the roof the rain would penetrate and eventually cause the cob walls to deteriorate. The only thing to do for immediate protection was to cover the roof with a tarpaulin. On inspection it was found that the beams had crumbled from the effect of woodworm. These would all have to be replaced before the new thatch could be put on. So restoring the cottage was going to take much longer than had first been thought.

During a dry spell we were able to remove the tarpaulin and start stripping off the old thatch. This was a very dirty job, the dust from it penetrated everything. As we pulled off the old straw and reeds we packed it into the trailer which was hitched to the back of my small car, then did a shuttle service to and fro up the hill to the disused gravel pit. As the trailer was unloaded the old thatch was tipped straight onto a bonfire which was situated in the centre of the gravel pit. The fire was kept going for several days, burning

93

down to just a smoulder at night. Not all the thatch was burnt as we saved samples of it to show the various materials used. These included ordinary straw which comprised the main layer and had been there about ten years. Beneath this were reeds and rushes from the water meadow, some of which were still green, pieces of bracken, bunches of coarse grass and heather, all having been added over the years as patching. In places we found the heather fixed to the purlins and rafters with thick tarred cord. Also amongst the straw were a variety of iron-spikes used in securing the woodwork.

The rafters, made from larch, were let into a wall plate, which was a half round larch pole running the length of the wall with the cob carried over the top to hold the roof down. The purlins consisted of split oak branches, very irregular in shape, which were spiked to the rafters. Eventually the entire roof was stripped off leaving only the cob walls standing. This gave the impression that the cottage was a complete ruin.

Arthur took advantage of a long dry spell of weather to start work on the new upright roof timbers. He decided to erect the rafters at a steeper angle to enable the upper room to be restored once again.

Unfortunately, whilst nailing in the very first one he hammered his thumbnail. For ten minutes or so it was numb and he carried on working, but gradually the feeling came back and the pain was excruciating eventually turning into a sickening throb as the blood gathered behind the nail. He tried hard to pierce the nail to relieve the pressure but could not do so and as it was the weekend he had to wait until Monday to see the doctor. Arthur said when the doctor saw it he exclaimed, "Oh good, I haven't had one of those for a long time," whereupon he produced a little spirit lamp which he filled with white spirit. According to Arthur some of the spirit ran down the side of the lamp onto the doctor's desk so that when he lit it the flame ignited the spilt spirit which in turn set fire to some papers on his desk. When order was restored the doctor used the lamp to heat a kind of needle with which he singed a hole through Arthur's nail. At once the blood welled up and gave instant relief.

Slowly the roof began to take shape and eventually was ready for thatching. We were lucky to be fitted in between two other bookings so there was no long wait. The master thatcher did not come himself but left it in the very good hands of his young apprentice. It was to be his first time thatching a complete roof by himself. He did an excellent job, in fact he was so painstaking that he ran out of his allotted time and his boss came along and finished it off. But to be truthful the piece that he did looked shoddy compared to the professional work of the young lad, who incidentally was very proud of his first roof.

I wanted to leave the thatch exposed on the inside but I did not realize that the first layer of straw is pushed well down into the rafters, leaving a rough untidy finish with long ends of straw hanging down and pieces of chaff falling to the floor. This is done to give a firm base for the outer layer of thatch otherwise it would slip off. Reluctantly we boarded in the beams and rafters, but when it was done it certainly looked neat and tidy, and the white paint resembled the lath and plaster of the original ceiling.

It was whilst working on the roof that we discovered a piece of paper stuck to the wall with the name ROSE COTTAGE written on it. We assumed that it must have been the name of the cottage when it was the home of foresters.

When the cottage was eventually finished with new thatch and restored upper room we thought it a good opportunity to give the old cabin back its original name of ROSE COTTAGE to continue its life after the restoration. A very appropriate name in many ways the cob walls outside were washed in rose pink and there were rose trees all around the building, some of which were of a very old variety.

We were not surprised that the mice found their way through the wire netting and into the thatch, attracted by the grains of corn still remaining in the wheatstraw used for the thatch. They would climb up the branches of the trees and onto the roof, and being so small could squeeze through the holes of the wire, burrowing their way into the space between the thatch and the ceiling board.

When sitting quiet in the upper room you could hear the patter of their little feet as they scampered to and fro. But we were surprised one day to hear the scratching of much bigger feet, and discovered by keeping a close watch on the cottage roof that a pair of squirrels had found their way in also. Before we could find exactly where they got in they did considerable damage to that particular piece of thatch. We eventually found a little area of rusted wire making a small hole through which they had gained access. Normally the squirrels live in the big yew tree behind the cottage where they have a drey and rear their babies each year. Looking down onto the cottage roof they probably thought that it was a much more desirable residence. It was a game of patience watching to see both squirrels leave the roof to go foraging before temporarily repairing the wire. The damage was such that the thatcher had to come back and patch the hole. The rain had already seeped through, staining the white boarding beneath.

The restored upper room proved to be very useful, a place to store moulding for picture frames, paintings, portable easels, and all the bits and pieces that go with oil painting. I had a lovely big knee hole desk which Arthur constructed in situ. This was the only way to do it as it would have been impossible to get a complete desk up the ladder stairway which was the only means of access to the upper room. By talking to some of the local foresters we discovered that this type of stairway was used in many of the old cottages and was sometimes situated outside to save space in the tiny interior.

In wintertime it was cosy to light a log fire in the big inglenook. It was however rather unpleasant when the fire was first kindled as the chimney smoked terribly making it necessary to have either the window or door slightly open to cause a draft to keep it clear. When the chimney had really warmed up the smoke rose freely. In the old days the fire was kept alight night and day so that the chimney never cooled down. Often the only means of cooking was by a pot hanging from a chain over the fire. Many open fireplaces had baking ovens in the side wall, as did Rose Cottage. It was thought that an oven heated by wood baked better bread than iron ovens attached to kitchen ranges which tended to harden and brown the surface of the bread before the heat had penetrated the centre of the dough. The method of heating a brick oven was to light a fire of faggot wood or logs inside it. When the wood had burnt clear the fire was raked out and the oven door closed tightly for half-an-hour before the baking began. The bread baked by the forester would probably have been made from flour ground in one of the New Forest mills.

Sides of bacon and hams were also hung up the chimneys to be cured by the smoke of Forest turf or gorse wood. Many of the foresters possessed the common or turbury which enabled them to dig peat from the Forest for their fires and peat stoves. These stoves were made of cast iron and resembled the wood-burning stoves of today.

We did quite a lot of cooking over the cottage fire whilst I was compiling my book, *New Forest Cookery*. Some of the recipes needed to be cooked in the original way to be sure of the results though most of them could be achieved on a modern stove.

At one time the forester and peasant had an abundance of food at their disposal in the way of game, berries and nuts, wild herbs, fungi, and of course rabbits. Even to this day local rabbits are always available in New Forest butcher shops during the season, the season being when there is an 'r' in the month.

The combination of thick cob walls and thatched roof provide an insulation to suit any weather. The inside of the cottage is cool in summer and warm in winter. We find the upper room, immediately beneath the thatch, very cosy and draught-free. Unfortunately the nearness of the straw produces a mouse-like smell, especially when the cottage is closed up for any length of time. However, I overcome this by placing little bowls and baskets of pot-pourri on the shelves and window-sills.

In late summer I pick the fruit of the quince tree which is now producing five or six fruits each season. Two or three of these placed on the sill in the little alcove window fills the air with a sharp fresh fragrance which drifts upwards to the room above. The smell and taste of the quince is so strong that it is necessary to use only one fruit to flavour an apple tart or preserve. Another tree which contributes a unique flavour to cooking, not with its fruit but its leaves, is the bay. At one time the forester always had a bay tree growing near his cottage, believing that it would keep away evil. There is still a bay tree growing in the garden beside Rose Cottage; nearby too is a tall yew which has also survived the years. Rose Cottage itself will survive many more years as one of the few remaining examples of an original New Forest cabin for it has now been made a listed building.

ೞ

11 Products of the Forest

THE FOREST HAS MANY PRODUCTS to offer in one way or another. From olden times to this day the forester has taken advantage of this and turned them to good use. Apart from food, rabbits, hares, wild berries and fungi, which were all available to the peasant, there were materials such as heather, bracken, timber and peat. With one or two exceptions these items are still enjoyed by the forester and commoner of today.

Heather in former times was incorporated into the thatch of forest cottages. We discovered this when our own cottage roof was stripped, for beneath the top layer of straw was heather together with reed from the meadow! Although not used for cottages today it is ideal for thatching the roofs of bird-tables, being found less desirable than straw by the birds for pulling out at nesting time.

When the leaves cover the Forest gardens in autumn there is a need for brooms, and heather is an excellent material to use for making besoms. Birch is another alternative but is rather stiff compared to heather which is pliable and sweeps the leaves from the flower borders without disturbing the ground beneath too much. Also it does not need the preparation which birch requires in the way of seasoning and steaming before being attached to the handles.

Another important use for heather is drainage; for this it has to be cut and compressed into bales. At a certain time of the year the machines can be seen cutting the acres of flat heathland alongside the main Ringwood-Cadnam road. Lyndhurst High Street is one of the locations where this form of drainage was introduced. As there is no way of diverting water between houses, heather sub-base drainage will permit the water to travel to a lower point where it can be dealt with.

When the heather is in full bloom the time is right to pick it for winter decoration. Tied into bunches and hung with the flowers downwards it will dry out and retain its colour. In winter the heather may then be arranged in vases, and sprigs can be placed in the log basket, or if you wish just leave the bunches hanging as they are.

Bracken can also be dried for winter decoration but by a different method. Pick the fronds in the autumn when they have just turned golden and are still moist and flat before they curl and crinkle. Place the sprays between newspaper and put under the carpet or rug and leave until Christmas. By this time they will have dried out and can then either be left natural or sprayed silver and gold for the festive season. In the autumn bracken is also collected to provide bedding for the animals.

Bracken and heather, together with other Forest vegetation, will produce dyes. The beautiful colours of the Forest – the mellow greens, sharp yellows, golds, browns and blues – can all be transferred into natural dyes. By gathering heather and gorse flowers, bracken tips, rush flowers, fir cones, blackberries and sloes and even bark from fallen trees (do not take bark from any living tree as it will damage them) and boiling them up to extract the dye you can make the colour of your choice. Bracken, gorse, and heather produce yellow, rush flowers gold, and ash bark olive-green, blackberries and sloes greyish-blue, whilst fir cones produce a dark brown. I can confirm the success of these dyes as I experimented with most of these mentioned colours on natural wool. The result was a range of subtle shades which I knitted up into a cape which also doubles as a bed cover.

Gorse is another versatile bush with many uses apart from providing food for the ponies. In springtime it spreads its yellow mantle over the open heathland of the Forest and fills the surrounding air with a coconut scent. Only the pollen can be gathered by the bees the nectar being secured inside the cups of the golden flowers. By gathering the flowers complete with their nectar a sweet and fragrant wine can be brewed. Juliette had a favourite recipe which she used for making a gorse drink, bottles of which she took to Augustus John who named it 'gorse champagne'.

The gorse bush also provides a home for several of the smaller birds to nest in, such as linnets, stonechats, and of course the shy and rare Dartford Warbler which we are fortunate in having on Hampton Ridge. An animal which hates gorse is the squirrel, for obvious reasons, so each year we tie a bunch of it around the trunks of the apple trees. This denies the squirrels access to the apples which we can now enjoy ourselves. The wood of the gorse has always been burnt by the forester. It was collected from the Forest, tied into bundles and stored for the winter. It is said that gorse wood burns with a yellow flame, reminiscent of its glorious golden flowers.

In spring the pale pink blossom of the wild apple adorns the Forest. For our May-time wedding we decorated the church with it. Later in the year there is an abundance of tiny apples which fall upon the Forest floor but are too sour to tempt the animals. If gathered up they will make a tart jelly that is very agreeable with cold pork.

Every year we pick blackberries for wine and jam making. Arthur makes the wine whilst I do the jam. The advantage with Forest blackberries is they are free from dust, growing as they do amongst the fresh bracken and often overhanging a stream and, most importantly, free from chemical sprays.

For making wine quite a few pounds of blackberries are needed. During one particularly good summer with days of hot sunshine which produced clusters of ripe juicy berries we set out to gather as many as we could. We trampled through bracken and brambles, and sometimes waded in the stream to secure the big clusters otherwise out of reach. When our baskets were full we covered them with bracken fronds to keep them fresh. The days that followed were spent making wine and afterwards attending to the fermenting must until eventually it was ready to go into the cask where it would stand for several months before being bottled off.

In the autumn the blackthorn bushes are dotted with dark sloes. Though small they are a decorative fruit with a bluish bloom. Unlike the sweet blackberries, sloes are too sour to eat raw and will dry up the mouth. However, they make a very palatable jelly to accompany cold meat, and also a very pleasant wine by filling a bottle with alternate layers of sloes and brown sugar.

A wide range of edible fungi is also found in the New Forest from the common mushroom to the lesser known such as chanterelle, blewits and puffballs. The little button mushrooms have brownish caps and can be eaten raw when freshly picked. The green-skinned puffballs which grow in the oak and beech woods are delicious fried with bacon. The violet-coloured blewits are a great favourite of the gypsies and at one time were often included in their stews when they lived on the Forest. The golden chanterelle can be found from summer till autumn in woodlands, and can be identified by its fragrance resembling that of apricots. We were delighted to find this colourful fungus growing under the birch trees on the bank beside our Abbots Well garden. Chanterelle can either be fried in butter or boiled in salted water and served on toast.

At one time, truffles, a subterranean species of fungus, could be found in the Forest. They were detected by scent using specially trained dogs or pigs. The latter were partial to the truffles themselves and often devoured the fungi before the pig-keepers could rescue them. Truffles are probably still growing in the Forest today, and no doubt the pigs turn them up when they are let out at pannage time to eat the acorns.

One of the last fruits of the year to be gathered from the Forest are the chestnuts. Clusters of nuts in prickly green jackets fall from the tall trees and scatter over the ground. Sometimes the green husks do not burst open so it is advisable to take a strong pair of gloves for protection as well as a basket when chestnutting.

Before we discovered Hasley Enclosure our former place for nutting was on the edge of the Forest where it drops away to meet the farmland in the valley. Situated there was the remains of an estate criss-crossed with paths that once were rhododendron walks now so overgrown it was like a jungle. One of these paths opened out into a clearing and there, set in a large circle, were several Grecian statues – all that remained of a once beautiful garden of a large country house now fallen into desolation as the Forest closes in from all sides. Leaving the statues and continuing along the track you would eventually come upon two very large chestnut trees. Being in such a remote and overgrown location few people knew of their existence and for several years we had the whole crop to ourselves. One year the nuts were full of worms, not realizing this at first we placed a bowl of them beside the fire ready for roasting. It was not until several days later we discovered that the worms had evacuated the nuts and taken up residence in various parts of the room. We found them inside books, and one had bored its way into the centre of a set of cork table mats.

ଔ

Fuel for his fire was something the forester enjoyed from the Forest by possessing the common of Turbary. This meant that he was entitled to cut turf for burning but when doing so had to cut one and leave two so as to ensure that this piece of Forest would not be stripped and that it would grow again. This entitlement is claimed by only one or two today. Another common right known as Estovers entitles the commoner to an allocation of firewood which is assigned in cords, this is an old-fashioned measure, one cord being approximately 128 cubic feet. This is cut and made ready by the Forestry Commission for collection by the registered commoner but it must be burnt in his own cottage.

Fuel for the fire which can be collected from the Forest today, without possessing the common of Turbary or Estovers, comes in the form of fir cones. These lie on the ground beneath the fir trees and, if gathered when dry, will open out and are ideal for lighting the fire or rekindling a dying one. In some of the enclosures the very tall firs and pines produce giant cones which I feel are too decorative to burn. They look very well heaped in a scuttle beside the fire, or two or three scattered in a bowl or flat round basket as a table decoration. At Christmas these big cones can be sprayed silver or gold, stood on end with a coloured candle in the top and a holly surround. Set in the centre of the Christmas dinner table they add a festive touch.

Other timber is sold by the Forestry Commission on a commercial basis. Different woods are used for various purposes such as pulping, fencing, and at one time the firs for pit-props. Some of the very tall pines in the Arboretum were cut down specially to be used as radar masts. In certain areas of the Forest where bombing occurred during the war many trees contain shrapnel, and this in the past has made difficulties when being cut at the saw mills.

During the winter months the woodmen are busy cutting down the hardwoods. When these trees are being felled it provides an opportunity to see their ages as they lie on the ground. Around the surface of the fresh cut trunk are a series of rings running symmetrically around the centre pith, so by counting the rings the age of the tree can be ascertained, one ring a year.

Whilst strolling through the wooded glades I have on occasions smelt woodsmoke and there in a clearing would be a row of iron kilns, all billowing smoke. For a while they were burning in Sloden Enclosure and this was visible from my kitchen window. The puffs of grey smoke drifted up through the trees and were mistaken by some people for forest fires. It was in fact charcoal burning which until recent years was still carried out in the New Forest but came to an end with the restriction on the felling of hardwoods.

It was one of the oldest industries in the Forest and dated back to the days before the Romans came. Apart from one or two modifications making charcoal was carried out in almost the same manner as in ancient times. Over the centuries this product of the woodlands has been widely used in many ways especially in the chemical industry.

The last time we saw charcoal burners in the forest was inJanuary 1968. It was a cold day with hazy sunshine as Arthur and I walked in an enclosure at Godshill. We could smell the burning wood and eventually came to a clearing where several iron kilns were smoking. There too were stacks of logs along the whole length of the iron kilns. We discovered that the two charcoal burners were brothers John and Ben Carter and that for years they had travelled around the woodlands of the south making charcoal. They had two caravans which was their accommodation on the various sites where their work took them.

The process of making the charcoal is very slow and calls for great patience. First the kiln has to be loaded – it will hold about two cords of wood - after which the fire is lit through an air hole into the kiln. This is followed by a long wait until the burning has finished and the kiln is ready for unloading, The charcoal has then to be put into bags ready for marketing.

Though a picturesque scene to come upon it is perhaps a good thing that charcoal burning is no longer carried out in the Forest. The amount of wood needed to keep the kiln fed would eventually have a devastating effect on the woodland.

ଔ

If you wish to capture a tiny bit of the Forest to last you through the winter then why not make a pot-pourri. There are so many things scattered on the forest floor which can be gathered up and dried for this purpose. The best time of the year to start your collection is late summer when the heather is out; small sprigs of the flowering heads will keep their colour for a long time. Gorse petals can be found anytime as somewhere there is always a gorse bush in bloom. Small pieces of golden bracken, brown seed clumps from the reeds, alder catkins, and the aromatic catkins from the bog myrtle will all blend together. Autumn will bring the nuts, beech mast, and the little flat underdeveloped chestnuts in rich brown. Even small pieces of their jackets when they have turned golden look attractive. The skins from the lovely olive-green puffballs dry very well; so too does the grey green lichen with its cobweb-like appearance. Tiny larch cones can be found whereever the Forestry woodmen have been cutting the low branches or where the wind has blown over an old tree. These I think are a must for the collection. Pine needles have a refreshing smell, and particularly good are the wood chippings left by the woodmen.

The fruits of autumn such as sloes and rose hips shrivel and dry but keep their colour. I also include the papery bark that peels off the pine trees. There is no end to the things you can gather from the forest floor.

It is essential to dry everything. To do so spread your ingredients out on tissue paper laid on a flat surface in an airy place. When everything has thoroughly dried out it can be mixed together and placed inbowls orbaskets. Ihave divided mine into two, onehalf of which is in the big bowl of a jug and bowl set whilst the other half is in a basket made for me by a gypsy and stands in the inglenook in Rose Cottage .

If left natural the aroma of the pot-pourri will be woody, but if you wish it can be enhanced by the addition of a few drops of appropriate oil which should be sharp rather than sweet to retain the atmosphere of the Forest.

12 Seasons in the Forest

WHEN THE FOREST AWAKES AFTER its winter rest the increasing warmth of the sun's rays encourages the growth of new vegetation. The buds on the trees open out and the delicate foliage of pale yellowish green is still covered with protective silky hairs. As spring advances the brightness of the green is a contrast to the otherwise sombre surroundings.

Already some of the very early blossoms are over, such as that of the blackthorn, which was in full bloom during the very cold days of March when the north-easterly winds were blowing. To country folk it is known as a 'blackthorn winter'. The blossom which coincides with the arrival of the cuckoo is the wild cherry. This most fragile of blooms has petals which float away at the slightest stir of the breeze, or even by the disturbance of bees collecting their first supply of nectar and pollen after the winter. In the nearby village of Woodgreen there are wild cherry trees in profusion. To me they are the real harbinger of spring. At one time there were several orchards of black cherry trees growing in the village and, when the fruit was ripening, bells were hung on the branches to frighten away the birds. These were called the 'cherry bells of Woodgreen'.

Early spring is when the Forestry Commission carries out its controlled burning. The old heather and the gorse which has grown tall and straggly is burnt off – both these plants will then throw new shoots which will flourish. This operation is carried out early in the year before the birds start nesting. However, when the winter has been mild and birds are breeding early, I doubt it is done soon enough.

As spring merges into summer there is another task to be carried out by the Forestry Commission and that is pulling up the ragwort. Every year this plant grows in clumps along the verges and is widespread across the whole Forest. Being poisonous to animals in its dying state it has to be removed. So, with stout gloves and a supply of plastic sacks, the Forestry men carry out their annual task.

During the summer various shows are held throughout the Forest with the 'New Forest' being the largest and most popular. Our local Fordingbridge Show has for several years now (apart from one break) been held at Godshill Cross. This is a good site with easy access and plenty of parking space. The show jumping begins early in the morning and continues throughout the day. Also there are heavy horses, Arabian breeds and horse-drawn carriages which are driven out into the Forest and on their return enter the ring to be judged. There are cattle, goats, sheep and donkeys too, not forgetting the dog show, and gun dog trials. In another field a clay pigeon shoot is in action, and an old threshing machine clatters away in the corner. Unlike the New Forest Show there is plenty of space to wander around and it is easy to get close to the displays in the craft and flower tents. Due to the heavy attendance the New Forest Show has been extended to two days and sometimes continues into a third day. Even so it is very crowded; many top names in show jumping are an attraction.

If, as summer lengthens, the weather has been warm and dry, the risk of forest fires is great. They are so easily started – a cigarette end or, if it is very hot, the thick bottom of a broken bottle will act as a magnifying glass and cause an outbreak. A forest fire can be very serious if the peat beneath burns as it will then travel underground and be difficult to put out. A story related to me by a forester was that in former days if they wanted to increase their grazing a delayed fire was started by an ingenious method, the manner of which I will not divulge for obvious reasons. Having set a kind of fuse the forester concerned would retire to the pub for the evening whereupon he would remark upon leaving that "he had better go and see how the fire was getting on." There have been one or two fires breaking out around Abbot Well, the circumstances being very suspicious. They happened in the dead of night when there should not have been anyone around to drop cigarette ends, or sun to give heat, and they were in very inaccessible places for the fire brigade to reach.

It is always a relief when the Forest is very dry to see the rain whether it be a brief storm or steady drizzle. If the rain comes from the south east it is known in this part of the forest as 'Woodfidley' or, as the locals would say, 'Oodfidley rain'. Woodfidley is a wood of fine old beeches to the east of Brockenhurst. When the rain does come from that direction it is sure to rain all day, or at least that is what the foresters will tell you and they are usually right.

Not only has Abbot Well the wild Forest before it but, on the Blissford side as it drops into the valley, there are several meadows which are left to grow for hay. These fields belong to commoners and therefore remain in their natural state with wild flowers growing, not poisoned by sprays and chemical fertilizers which kill the flowers and produce a monotonous green grass. In the village of Blissford is the farm which supplies our milk. The cows – a handsome herd of Guernseys and Jerseys – graze amongst wild flowers, some rare, in fields which have never been touched by sprays. Until recently the milk was delivered by the farmer who was in his eightieth year but always immaculate in polished boots and gaiters. When he retired the round was taken over by his son Leonard Sevier. Sometimes when the yield is low or a cow is about to calf we have to wait for our delivery until after second milking. Being natural milk rather than pasteurised we have it almost straight from the cow – it could not be fresher. When the milk arrives it is topped with a thick rich cream which can be taken off and used over fruit on in coffee.

When haymaking time comes the air is aromatic especially if the weather is warm and the sun shining. Long hours are spent cutting the hay whilst the conditions are good, then a few days later it has to be tossed. When the hay is dry it is loaded onto trailers which are then pulled up the hill by tractor.

Occasionally at that time of year there is one of those perfect evenings when the air is still and warm, and the bats flit and dive over the garden. I recall one such evening as we walked home from visiting friends at Blissford. A full moon shone over Hampton Ridge and the warm air was heavy with the smell of hay and honeysuckle. As we turned into the lane there were standing beside the wells, looking mysterious in the pale silver light, the silent figures of two black donkeys; then, on entering the garden we saw shining from thebankbeside the gate two glow-worms – an experience thatlingers in the memory for a long while.

Our first autumn atAbbots Well was one to be long remembered. By mid-September there were signs that the fall was going to be early. The bracken was already tipped with bronze and the birch trees were studded with yellow amongst the green. The mornings were crisp and patches of mist rose over the meadows at night. By October the surrounding Forest was ablaze with colour from the golden-brown bracken that surrounded the wells and stretched over the hills, to the glorious hues massed together in the trees of Hasley Enclosure and Sloden.

One often wonders what brings about this beautiful display of colour. It is due to the fact that the leaves of many of our trees and shrubs cannot stand the frosts of winter; being of no further use they are thrown off, but not before the many useful substances they contain whilst in their green state are reabsorbed. This being done the leaves now contain nothing but useless residues and a small amount of waste matter. There is a chemical change taking place in the chlorophyll bodies which causes the leaves to lose their green colour and become yellow. So with this happening all over the Forest we get our beautiful colours of autumn. How early the tints begin to appear depends on the atmospheric conditions. When the September air has been dry and cool they appear very early, but usually later if early summer is warm and moist.

That particular autumn was spectacular and lasted well into November; the.weather was mellow, and we were able to walk in the deep Forest as it was so dry underfoot. Studley was especially enchanting most of the trees were oaks and their leaves which had turned to a pale yellow, reflected the glow from the golden bracken beneath. On the ground there were various types of fungi, including the scarlet fly-agaric, which gave a bright contrast to the russet surroundings.

The thick clusters of holly berries outside the kitchen window were now a pale orange, and the boughs of the hazel tree that grew beside it were heavy with nuts. Squirrel was frantically busy picking and burying them all over the lawn. Looking around the Forest it was noticeable that every, tree or bush was thick with fruit, and the oak trees were shedding so many acorns that foresters were worried about the cattle and ponies as too many eaten by them can prove disastrous.

Although acorns and beechmast are bad for ponies they make very good food for pigs. The common of Mast or Pannage, when the pigs can be turned onto the Forest, occurs in late September until the middle of November. I always like to see them foraging amongst the leaves when I am walking in the Forest. At one time pigs were kept in sties adjoining the farmhouse or in a small compound surrounded by high earth hedges. They too were turned on to the Forest in the autumn to feed on the fallen acorns and beechmast. It was said that due to the nuts in their diet the ham assumed a pleasant flavour which was found only in the pigs of the New Forest.

Whilst the pigs are having their autumn feed the bees and other winged insects are stocking up on their winter provisions. The ivy, being one of the last to bloom, is naturally a great attraction. On a sunny day if you walk beneath an ivy-clad tree you will hear overhead the endless buzzing of numerous winged insects, bees and flies; even butterflies join in all trying to secure the sweetness from the liffle rosettes of yellow-green flowers. Later in the evening at dusk the nocturnal insects, beetles and moths arrive for their share.

CS

During our early days at Abbots Well, bracken was used extensively by the forester for animal bedding. Every autumn it was harvested and then stored in the form of ricks which were thatched with reeds to keep out the rain. At that time of year Len Witt could be seen on the side of Windmill Hill cutting the bracken with a hook and then carrying it home in a rope sling on his back. Another forester neighbour cut his bracken from Abbots Well Green and Chilly Hill. He loaded it all onto a cart whilst the pony stood patiently until the bracken was piled high and ready to take home.

The last time we saw bracken being harvested in this way was in 1983 at Brook. It was a bright sunny day and the autumn colours were at their best. As we came over the hill and down towards the village our attention was caught by the sight of a little black mare standing in the shafts of a cart loaded with bracken just off the side of the road. Close by was a forester with a scythe cutting the bracken. We stopped for a word with him, he said he had been doing it for years but the mare was soon to be retired although she was still able to do a good day's work. As he put the last bundle on top of the cart he said he was going to take it home and come back for another load in the afternoon. There is a vegetable grower living in a neighbouring village who always cuts bracken in the autumn to use for covering tender plants as protection against frost.

November 5th is a night for keeping alert in the Forest for, although the bonfire and fireworks parties are well organized, occasionally an odd spark carried on the wind will start a heath fire. I recall a small bonfire party we had ourselves. For days we collected pieces of gorse wood and hedge trimmings from the garden and stacked it by the forest gate. On bonfire night we took it outside onto the boggy ground where we normally burn the garden rubbish; well away from the thatched cottage roof. It was a lovely evening with a clear sky and very little wind. We hung a lantern over the gateway to illuminate the way until the firelight took over. By the time our friends arrived the flames were well away. As the fire burnt clear a rosy glow lit up the gorsebushes and penetrated the shadow. Turning for a moment from the fire, I saw standing in the glow a grizzled grey mare and behind her the silhouette of another smaller pony. For some time they stood gazing into the fire, the flames reflecting in their eyes. Were they attracted by the warmth or were they perhaps thinking that they had come upon a gypsy camp fire such as they remembered from days now passed? After a while they turned and moved away as silently as they had arrived. Gradually the flames died down until only the embers were left glowing and the light that shone was that of the full moon rising above the birch trees over the wells.

oB

As autumn drew to a close it was obvious that it would be remembered as the year of the holly. Mid-November showed the forest ablaze with holly berries in all hues from orange, vivid scarlet, crimson to darker vermilion. Not a few berries but thick clusters which predominated over the dark green leaves. Trees that before had produced only the odd berry were now excelling themselves. On November the 26th each year permits are issued for a fee by the Forestry Commission to those who wish to cut holly for commercial purposes. It always annoys me to see how much damage is done to the trees by the holly gatherers who cut it to sell in the neighbouring markets for they often hack the top off the tree just to reach a few sprigs. They then leave the stripped branches lying on the ground together with discarded pieces of twine.

A neighbouring farmer related how he and his father had an area allocated where they were allowed to pick holly, having paid their dues. They would then take it by train to Nine Elms Station in London. On one occasion he remembers having twelve truck-loads. They then sold it straight from the trucks to the barrow boys but they had to watch carefully for very often as they were selling from the front the holly was being stolen from behind.

ᏯᏃ

Winter as well as the other seasons in the Forest has its own joys, for one thing it brings the wild geese. One cold December afternoon I heard their unmistakable call and, hurrying outside, I was just in time to see about thirty geese flying across the cheerless sky. What an exciting feeling it was to imagine oneself for a few brief moments in the open spaces of Siberia, the breeding grounds of these wild visitors. All too soon they had gone, disappeared into the mist of that grey December afternoon. As I turned to go my attention was taken by the appearance of a graceful hen harrier gliding buoyantly over the heathland towards Windsmore Pond but that too was soon lost in the mist.

The next morning I once again heard the cry of wild geese but this time there were several skeins flyingvery high. I later discovered that they were white-fronted geese and had landed in the water meadows of the Avon Valley. This lovely valley which runs alongside the New Forest is a favourite haunt of many species of wildfowl in the season – wigeon, pintail, pochard, teal, Bewick's swans and numerous others. All through January and February the geese continued to come and go. Some days as many as a thousand would arrive, their yapping calls filling the air as they turned and dipped and then climbed again trying to land but far too nervous to do so at the first attempt.

The winter frosts turned the Forest into a wonderland edging the brown bracken with lace and studding the branches of the trees with diamonds. The bogs all froze and Windsmore Pond iced over, but the wells never freeze. Now that the frosts had brought the leaves down, leaving the branches of the trees stark and bare against the sky, things were revealed that had been hidden during the summer months. The witch's brooms became visible on the birch trees, old nests and squirrels' dreys were conspicuous, and tufts of mistletoe could be seen on some trees. There was a whitebeam tree growing on Old Sloden Hill which had branches of mistletoe sprouting from it. It is a parasitic plant, feeding on the sap of the tree on which it grows. We made a pilgrimage every year at Christmas time to pick a sprig. Recently the tree was blown over, at first the mistletoe went on growing but as the tree died and there was nothing left for the mistletoe to feed on so it died too.

On recollection, the winters in our early days at Abbots Well seemed much colder, with a memorable white Christmas one year in particular. The frost often came with the moons and, during one of these spells when the ground was white and crisp, Arthur and I walked across the Forest to Windsmore Pond. It looked mysterious with the ice shimmering in the moonlight. We disturbed a snipe that was squatting in the marshes, and it flew off worrying into the night. Turning away from the pond we walked past some old foxes' earths, and with the full moon lighting up the distant hills we came upon a herd of black cattle standing and lying amongst the furze. We saw a pair of new-born calves and wondered how they could survive such a cold night, but they seemed happy enough.

That same year just at dusk on Christmas Eve fine powdery snow flakes filled the air. Christmas Day dawned on a white world with a light dusting of snow covering everything. On the morning of Boxing Day it began to snow heavily and the wind suddenly blew whipping up the powdery snow and sticking it fast against the tree trunks, and banking the sides of the roads. The dovecote in the garden rocked to and fro, and the pigeons perched on top had to battle their way down the thatch to reach the shelter inside. The blizzard raged until mid-afternoon, leaving behind a carpet of snow. The wind dropped as suddenly as it had blown up and once more everything was quiet.

The sky was still heavy with threatening snow as we set out for a walk to Hasley. Flocks of redwing and fieldfare were searching for berries on the holly trees along the way. We must have missed the track as we found ourselves on the open moorland, ankle deep in heather and snow. As we reached the fringe of the fir woods I stepped into one of the notorious Forest bogs hidden beneath the snow. My right leg sank into it up to my knee; with difficulty I managed to pull it out, only to find my boot and trouser-leg covered in a layer of thick sticky clay. It was useless to try and wipe it off, the only thing to do was to let it dry. Disregarding it we continued on our way until we came to a badger sett. It was situated in a wood on a slope sheltered from the blizzard so not very much fresh snow had penetrated, but there was a covering from the previous fall. Around several of the holes were a number of badger footprints and discarded bedding dug out on the snow proving that the badgers were in residence and had been out since the snow.

I would have liked to have stayed and watched over the sett but we had not come prepared to stand for any length of time in such conditions. We would have needed rugs around our shoulders as the temperature was already below freezing; it was beginning to snow again and we had a long walk home before us.

As best we could we followed the twisty path down through the woods leading to the track past the farmhouse. Then by the time we climbed the long hill to Abbots Well it was quite dark and snowing steadily, and our faces were stiff from the biting east wind. As we reached our cottage we could see through the window the warming sight of a blazing log fire, and the colourful lights of the Christmas tree. Inside my mother had ready a pot of tea and a plate of hot mince pies.

The weather continued severe with hard frosts and more snow falling. The ice on Windsmore Pond became so thick that people were able to skate, and children in gay sweaters and woolly hats made a colourful scene against the wintry background.

Walking once again in Hasley Enclosure we found the going very tiring, the snow being so deep it was necessary to lift our feet high between each step. However, the beauty of the scenery made us forget these discomforts. Along the sides of the track the fir trees were laden and in places the lower branches were touching the ground. It was a silent world with all sound being muffled by the snow. There were numerous animal trails, some of which were intrig~ung, such as the one we came upon of a rabbit and a fox. The light prints of the rabbit were followed by the heavier indents of a fox just behind and slightly to one side. It was left to one's imagination as to whether the fox was stalking the unsuspecting rabbit, or if it was two separate incidents with the prints coinciding. We followed the trail for some distance until it eventually vanished into the undergrowth. That was an exceptionally hard winter with the snow laying for weeks which caused great hardship and casualties to the wildlife.

ೞ

The last event of the year in the foresters' calendar takes place on Boxing Day morning when the annual New Forest Point-to-Point races are held. Raced across one-and-a-half to three miles of open forest it is the only authentic Point-to-Point in the country. The start is kept secret until the day; only the finish is known in advance. This is to ensure that no one can ride the course beforehand. There are various classes; for example, children's, young commoners, veterans, ladies and beginners. These are particularly gruelling races run over rough and treacherous ground under varying weather conditions. But the Forest folk, commoners and agisters are very skilful in handling their mounts over the wild heath as it is all part of their routine to round up and tend the animals, therefore they usually do well in their class.

There are no bookmakers allowed but a Shetland pony with money-box on his back is led around collecting donations. The trophies for the winners are on display in the public address system caravan. Ponies and riders gallop across the Forest and finish covered in mud but having enjoyed every minute.

The following story was told to me by a commoner about his mare which happened after the New Forest races when they traditionally met at the local inn to discuss the day's events and celebrate their wins: "Having celebrated rather too much I was unable to stand once outside in the cool air. Although I cannot remember it was related to me afterwards that my fellow revellers hoisted me on to the back of the little mare who was tied up and patiently waiting. I immediately slumped forward over her neck and fell asleep. They gave her a sharp slap on the rump and sent her going. Apparently the little mare found her way home and pushing the garden gate open, walked up the path and threw me off outside the door at the same time whinnying loudly for my wife to come out and find me."

A little far-fetched do you think? But on the other hand there is no knowing the intelligence of these devoted and loved animals. The seasons now have completed a full turn but nature does not stand still, for already there are catkins on the hazel trees outside my kitchen window, and underground in the Forest badger cubs are being born. Within a month or two the first foals will be running with the mares, then we shall be looking for the swallows and listening for the cuckoo. Once more spring is on its way.

Postscript

OVER THE YEARS THERE HAVE been numerous changes in the Forest, perhaps the most notable being the closing of Forest tracks to motorists. It was once possible to drive along these and camp where you wished. There was a time when campers erected their tents on the green at Abbots Well, a favourite spot because of the supply of water from the wells. I have on occasions seen these campers doing their washing in the open tub from which the animals drink. Thankfully now that is a thing of the past. There are specially sited parks where the motorists can leave their cars and walk, and for the campers and caravaners there are sites in various parts of the Forest.

A change of policy by the Forestry Commission which I think is sad is that they now partake in the widespread use of chemical sprays in order to try and eradicate the bracken. Used now, I am sorry to say, without any warning to the public that a particular area has recently been sprayed. This summer at Abbots Well the Forestry Commission vehicle arrived at a quarter-to-seven every morning for a week and for several hours disgorged its evil smelling liquid over the heath just beyond our garden. Little did we think we would have to close our windows to keep out the obnoxious smell of chemical in the New Forest. In the past the bracken was swiped and the commoners cut and dried it to use as bedding for their animals.

Poison traps are also now used to control squirrels. I consider these unsuitable as I have personally witnessed them in other Forestry Commission plantations used in such a manner that did not prevent access to these traps by other creatures. When misused in this way and not properly supervised there is an indiscriminate killing of other wildlife. In my opinion the use of poison on any creature is cruel as it is not instantaneous and is bound to cause suffering.

Fortunately little has changed at Abbots Well – the birch trees around the wells are perhaps taller and the traffic a little noisier, but the ponies and cattle and donkeys still come and go up and down the lane, and the garden is nightly visited by badgers and foxes.

Sadly the beehives had to be removed from the garden due to the invasion of New Forest Blacks, a very aggressive strain of bee which is native to the Forest. They eventually overwhelmed our original docile brown Weavers and stung anyone who ventured too near to the hives, I was stung so many times that I eventually reacted badly so we reluctantly decided to give them up. We are still able to enjoy local honey though as there are several beekeepers nearby some of whom put their hives on the Forest amongst the heather in the summer.

Every spring we look forward to the return of the migratory birds. There have been flycatchers returning to a little nest box on the side of the cottage for as long as we can remember. The offspring have followed on from the original pairs as we were to discover one spring. On returning home from only a short absence one morning we found a pair of flycatchers lying dead on the verandah obviously having flown into the plate glass window. We were horrified, but to our amazement a few days later another pair arrived and took over the nest box; probably the fledgelings from last year which had found their way back. It is amazing that these tiny birds can fly all the way from Africa straight to the tiny nest box on the cottage.

By keeping a five-year diary we are able to see that the swallows return to the stable in the meadow at almost the same date every year. Through spring and summer they act as a weather indicator, if they dart low over the garden, just skimming over the tops of the hedges then there is bad weather on the way but, should they go soaring high in the sky to feed, then it will be fine.

The birds that over the winter have joined flocks and flown away to the fields return to the garden in the spring to find mates and build their nests. An indicator that the greenfinches are back is when the primrose heads start disappearing. I have watched these colourful little birds fly down to the flower border, snatch off a primrose and carry it back to their nest. This action they keep up until enough flower heads have been collected to completely line their nest. The chaffinches prefer the gossamer of fine spiders' webs to keep their babies warm. They meticulously search and gather them from around the window arches, sometimes flying back to the nest with long pieces of web trailing out behind them. It is amazing how they extricate the sticky thread from their beaks and weave it into the surrounds of the nest.

When the bluebells are in bloom at the far end of the garden the green hairstreak butterflies appear. Too numerous to count, these dainty little green butterflies spend their days flitting from one flower to another, sometimes resting to sun themselves before meeting with another and go spiralling up together out of sight against the blue sky.

All through the spring and summer the garden is visited by a variety of butterflies from the colourful Peacocks and Red Admirals to the small Orange Tips. But the harbinger of spring is always the Brimstone, its colour rivalling that of the primroses and wild daffodils. As summer lengthens we are sometimes honoured by a visit from a Grayling butterfly, probably blown into the garden from the Forest beyond. This is not a common species, and is found only on heathland around the time when the heather is in bloom. We can usually be sure of finding these butterflies – often in considerable numbers – on Old Sloden Hill. They are recognisable by their habit of closing their upper wings when resting, and leaning sideways so as not to cast a shadow. It is difficult to see the colour or pattern on the top of their wings as they bring them together immediately on landing. Very rarely does the grayling take nectar from the flowers but prefers to sip the resinous sap oozing from the pine trees.

It is still a delight early on a spring morning to hear the wild call of the curlews across the Forest and equally so the whirr of the nightjar as dusk approaches. These mysterious birds return every year to the heath beyond the garden where they can sometimes be seen sitting on the dead branch of a gorse bush silhouetted against the setting sun. Just before darkness falls on fine clear evenings of spring and summer one of these fern owls, as nightjars are sometimes called, will fly low over the garden in pursuit of its insect prey. Although just a shadowy form against the darkening sky it is easily recognisable by its erratic flight.

At the same time the bats are darting in all directions, also feeding on late flying insects. After wondering for years if they perhaps lived in the big open chimney of the old cottage I discovered one day that in fact they sleep in the roof. It was in daylight that I saw a bat fly under the thatch and vanish up into the eaves of the cottage. So at last my curiosity was satisfied.

The old ivy-covered tree by the landing window has long since gone – the victim of a gale – but the tawny owl must have found another home nearby as his eerie hoot can regularly be heard in summer and winter.

Not such welcome visitors to the garden were the hornets. Their presence became evident one evening when four of these large wasp like insects came buzzing through the kitchen window whilst I was jam-making. The next morning we could see there were several hornets coming and going under the eaves of the house so it was obvious that there was a nest in the roof. We contacted John Gulliver, a New Forest keeper who is very knowledgeable on the subject of hornets. If they are being a nuisance he will come and remove the nest complete with inhabitants and rehouse them in a tree somewhere in the Forest. But he advised us that as it was nearly the end of summer it would be better to leave the nest and occupants where they were as the workers die before the winter and only the queen survives and she will find somewhere new to breed again.

Over the years the deer have become much tamer. Sometimes as many as fifteen bucks with fine heads will be feeding in the meadow below the house in the early morning often staying on to sun themselves until something disturbs them. Then gracefully they will leap the fence and return to the Forest and the cover of the bracken.

More badgers did find their way to the garden and over the years have continued to do so. On occasions they have brought their cubs with them. The sow from a nearby sett is our most regular visitor; she is small and her ears are out of line so this, together with her limp (caused by a very stiff foreleg), makes her easy to recognise. She has become so accustomed to the noises and smells around the garden and house that she is quite relaxed. When she has finished the peanuts put out for her on the verandah she will come to the french window and look to see if anyone is coming with more food. You can open the door slowly whilst speaking softly to her, and she will take a biscuit or slice of bread from your hand. During the very dry weather of summer, when the sow was really hungry and unable to find worms which is her natural food, she would follow a trail of peanuts over the door step and into the room. We do not make a habit of this as she is a wild animal and it would be a mistake to make her too tame.

Over the past few years new laws have been made giving more protection to badgers and their homes. During the early seventies the Forestry Commission formed the Badger Protection Group for the purpose of monitoring the setts within the Forest. All Forest keepers became members, together with a limited number of people who have the welfare of the badgers at heart and were willing to give up their time to regularly visit and sit over the setts. Eventually we were able to become members of the group with our own setts to monitor and report on.

For a few years a small vixen visited the garden every evening at dusk. She first arrived on a warm evening in May, coming to the edge of the verandah via the back of the herbaceous border. As time went on she became very daring until eventually she would come within a few feet of us to retrieve a dog biscuit thrown to her. If she was leaving the garden and you called her she would turn and come back. One summer evening we were walking back across the Forest when we saw 'Uffa' as we called her, walking past the wells having just left the garden. We called to her, whereupon she immediately sat down dog-fashion on her haunches and watched us go through the gate into the garden. Five minutes later she was back on the lawn waiting for her supper. On some occasions if we had been out late we would return home and find her curled up asleep under the kitchen window.

Uffa and the badgers were good friends although they often had a confrontation; the fox then thought it prudent to retreat and keep her distance. Sadly, one night Uffa did not come for her supper and we never saw her again. With the precarious life they live it could have been one of a number of things – the hunt, a commoner's gun or a car.

Rose Cottage remains our studio and is still being visited by artists and gypsies just as it was all those years ago when Juliette lived there. Recently the cottage came into its own again when we held an art event which turned into a gypsy gathering. The occasion was an exhibition of my paintings. The evening of the opening was dreary with wind and rain, but inside the cottage was a blaze of colour with the glow of the paintings mingling with the flamboyant dress of the gypsies.

The Romanies had only arrived in Wiltshire that morning after a long slow journey from the Cotswolds. Anxious to see themselves and their fellow travellers in the paintings, they came to the cottage in a group. The paintings of bow-tops, big coloured horses and children around the campfire pleased the travellers. Laughter mingled with excited chatter, together with the colourful dress, floral skirts, gay headscarves, gold earrings, and the ribbons and bows in the children's hair cheered the evening.

Gazing down on the scene from her portrait on the wall was the old New Forest gypsy Eiza Cooper who in the past had been a regular caller at the cottage. How delighted she would have been had she known that her granddaughter and great granddaughter Jane and Donna Cooper followed in her footsteps by visiting the cottage. They came with a mutual friend to see where the old gypsy lady had spent so much of her time helping Juliette with her herbal remedies.

The cottage seems to have a magnetic attraction, drawing back those who have at some time lived there. Such a person arrived one Sunday morning, a very interesting lady who said she had been evacuated with her mother to the village from Southampton during the war after very heavy bombing raids. They were put into a caravan on Hyde Common but the same night a bomb intended for a nearby aerodrome fell not far off shattering the windows and making the caravan uninhabitable. Someone told them there was a small cottage at Abbots Well which was empty but could possibly be lived in. After hurried negotiations with the owner they moved in, made themselves comfortable and stayed for two years. The lady was able to tell us more details of the cottage as to how it was then - its size and exactly where the ladder stairway was, another piece of the cottage's mysterious past brought to light. Being a listed building there are certain conditions we have to follow. For example, we cannot alter the cottage in any way or add to it without permission. Recently when the thatch needed renewing it had to be done using long straw and without a high ridge. This is the way the roof would originally have been thatched when occupied by foresters.

Perhaps the most devastating change made was to the water meadow below the garden. Several years ago the owner decided to have it drained to improve the grazing for keeping a horse. The apple trees and willows were cut down, the raised bank under the dividing hedge was flattened and the roadside one removed leaving only the mature oaks and a few bramble bushes. The meadow was ploughed and drainage pipes buried in the ground and for several months it remained just an expanse of mud. Gone were the flowers and rushes, herbs and orchids; the following year brought a crop of fat hen which covered the whole field. This was sprayed with a poisonous chemical which ended any possibility of wild flowers blooming again in the meadow for a long time. However, during the last few years the pipes have become blocked and the meadow is gradually reverting to its former boggy self with a few more wild flowers appearing each spring, in particular one or two sprigs of the now quite rare ragged robin. The horse has long since gone, so the water flags can bloom without being crushed beneath restless hooves.

In the adjoining village of Blissford another meadow, lush with wild flowers, has also lost the trampling of hooves. Len Sevier, the farmer who supplied and delivered our milk, has retired and reduced his herd to a couple of house cows. We are no longer able to enjoy fresh natural milk from cows grazing on uncontaminated grass but have to endure pasteurized milk delivered every other day.

ℒ

We consider ourselves privileged and indeed lucky to live in such a winderful place surrounded as we are by beautiful landscape and a wealth of animal life. It is only natural, therefore, that we find ourselves increasingly protective towards such an environment. We have over the years endured changes in the management of the New Forest which have indeed been timely and much needed; I refer particularly to the exclusion of motor cars on Forest tracks. However, in present times, with the urge to produce profit and to make Government Departments pay their way, the commercial pressures on the New Forest are becoming increasingly worrying. One can only hope that public awareness of the need to protect our countryside will eventually lead to better understanding by those who manage our heritage.

ℒ